# THE POEMS W

## An Anthology
## of
## AIR FORCE POEMS

Eddy Coward

**Compiled and Edited**

**by**

**EDDY A. COWARD.**

ISBN 0 9530255 00

Dedication:-

Original calligraphy by L. J. Hay.

Design, Layout & Typesetting:-

E. B. Cachart.

Publishers:-

E.A. Coward. 5 Brocksford Avenue. Rayleigh. Essex. SS6 8RH.

E.B. Cachart. 4 Cottage Close. Heage. Derbyshire. DE56 2BS.

Printers:-

Esparto Digital Ltd. Slack Lane. Derby. DE22 3DS.

This anthology is dedicated

to the memory of

Seven Gallant Gentlemen

of the

49th Squadron, Bomber Command,

Cliff, Al, Pete and John,
Nick, Stan & Skipper – Don.

Killed in action – 11th April, 1944.

# INTRODUCTION

The day I conceived the idea of compiling this Anthology of Air Force Poems from around the world, I never envisaged it would take over 6 years to complete and that I would meet and correspond with so many wonderful people and make so many friends.

I am extremely grateful to everyone who has sent me their poems and suggestions, without your help this book would never have been possible and the wealth of your material has been overwhelming.

The multitude of poems, verses, songs and parodies that have been submitted to me over the years, added to my own private collection of over 300, has made it extremely difficult to select those that have the most appeal or are suitable for publication, (needless to say that a number were unprintable - but a joy to read!).

I hope my selection will cater for the tastes of all the readers and the verses will reflect the various moods and feelings of our poets. Whether they are jocular or sombre, lyrical or emotional, they were all written with great pride and a tribute to the days they served in their Air Force.

Included are a few poems that are not connected with our gallant aviators and ground staff, but I know I will be forgiven and you will enjoy reading *For The Fallen* by Lawrence Binyon in its entirety and also two masterpieces *Sepulchre Of Heroes* and *I Am Not There.*

It would be unfair to nominate my favourite poems because they are all my favourites. My compilation of Air Force poems would not be complete if I did not include John Magee's *High Flight* or his lesser known *Per Ardua. High Flight* was recited by the former President of the United States of America, Mr Ronald Regan during his dramatic speech on the Challenger tragedy in 1986. I visited John Magee's grave in Lincolnshire and was pleased to see that the first and last lines of *High Flight* are engraved on his headstone.

*Stand Those Three Towers* by Victor Standish epitomizes the welcome relief to many World War II aircrew sighting the landmark of the three towers of Lincoln Cathedral in the early morning light. Jim Davis kindly sent me his *High On The Velvet Mantle* which is engraved on the Royal Air Force International Monument at Plymouth. I would also mention *Where Are They* by Audrey Grealy and *What Think You Airman* by Dennis Hornsey, because they have a special message with so much feeling and conjure vivid pictures in one's mind.

My namesake, the late Sir Noel Coward, has given a civilian's eyeview with his *Lie In The Dark and Listen*, and I was very pleased to receive a copy of Mike Harding's poignant *Bombers Moon* which he has recorded on one of his many albums.

My own *Spirits In Flight* was written after an emotional visit to the derelict and deserted airfield at Fiskerton in Lincolnshire. It is my tribute to all the airmen and airwomen who served with 49 Squadron and to the memory of the aircrews who did not make the touch down at R.A.F. Fiskerton to the call of Bandlaw. In May 1995, it was my honour to read *Spirits In Flight* at the dedication of the 49 and 576 Squadron's memorial on Fiskerton airfield. *Spirits in Flight* is now engraved on a stainless steel plaque and mounted on a piece of Ancaster stone placed at the Fiskerton Airfield memorial.

My second poem, *A Flemish Field* I wrote following my visit to Sint Lenaarts in Belgium, the crash site of my late brother Pilot Officer Clifford Coward of 49 Squadron, R.A.F. Bomber Command. I was invited to attend a ceremony in Belgium in June 1994 for the unveiling of a memorial to 240 aircrew who were killed in action over Belgian soil, and the poem A *Flemish Field* was read in Flemish by the President of the N.S.B. and again in English by yours truly.

I salute the people who have written and composed the many poems and parodies, their penmanship portrays service life in peace and war in the Air Forces of the World. They have stirred nostalgic memories of a period in our lives that can never be repeated or recaptured. Above all, you can sense the camaraderie that strongly reflects from their verses.

Wartime aircrew who flew the killing skies of aerial warfare have my greatest respect and admiration. I have spoken with many such aircrew and note that whenever they speak of their Squadron, a note of pride enters their voice. Also, they always have this love-hate relationship with their aircraft. I feel proud to be so deeply involved with their poems and verses.

I am sure you will enjoy reading these Air Force poems that span nearly a century from *The Dying Aviator* written in 1908 through two world wars and many other conflicts and into the '90's with *My Thanks*, written by 11 year old Samantha Davis and *The Lancasters* by 10 year old Lindsay Ward, a new generation of young poets.

Now sit back, put your feet up and with a glass in your hand, savour

***The Poems We Wrote***

**Eddy Coward** **1997** **Rayleigh.Essex.**

# SEVEN GALLANT GENTLEMEN

**49 SQUADRON BOMBER COMMAND**

**LANCASTER LL899, B FLIGHT**

**R.A.F. FISKERTON, LINCOLNSHIRE**

**TARGET - AACHEN, GERMANY**

**KILLED IN ACTION - 11TH APRIL 1944**

*"Every April, Every Easter - I will remember"*

**Eddy Coward**

## SPIRITS IN FLIGHT

I saw them return, seven spirits in flight.
Engines fired by the sparks of night.
Lumbering, throbbing like a battered ghost.
So thankful for a friendly coast.

Glowing and gliding, it roars without sound.
The rubber screams, as it kisses the ground.
Perfect touch down, on a deserted plain.
Now a corn field, a field with no name.

Night after night, mission after mission.
Helmets, visors, masks and ammunition.
The Seven Sky Warriors from long past.
All knowing tonight, could be their last.

I hear the fields, alive with noise,
Filled with brave men, some are just boys,
I see them walk, in their suits of leather.
Slowly and proudly, they walked together.

Where their planes rose, to meet the foe.
Now the larks rise, from their nests below.
Down the runway, only peace is heard.
Save for the wind, and the song of a bird.

Time passes - January to December.
From Spring to Winter, the years drift on.
Every April, Every Easter - I will remember.
Cliff, Al, Pete and John - Nick, Stan and Skipper Don.

**Eddy Coward (1985)**

## THE FEW

Time passes, generations come and go,
Full fifty years can melt into a day,
But we will not be able to repay
The timeless debt we will forever owe.

The sky their battlefield, a dazzling blue,
Its airy silence shattered by the noise
Of fighters flown by men no longer boys,
Whose youth passed in a day - the gallant Few.

These old young men, exhausted, battle spent,
Whose will to stay alert, to live, to fight,
Held them unfaltering in their fearsome flight
Above the blossoming summer fields of Kent.

They fought their fear, they kept their courage still,
The friends they lost must be no more than names,
They put from mind the blood and death and flames,
And dreamed, in hope, of life, as young men will.

The years flow on, September passes by,
And sometimes, in these tranquil golden days,
My memory glimpses still the drifting haze
Of fading vapour trails across the sky.

**Audrey Grealy (1989)**

## EPITAPH (for F/Lt Jean "Peiker" Offenberg, D.F.C.)

Here, in the corner of an English shire,
Far from the homeland that he fought to save,
A Belgian pilot sleeps, who dying gave
His all, for all of England to admire.

Here was a warrior of the lonely sky,
Modest and brave, outstanding of his race,
Who winged the outer air with swallow's grace
To us it hardly seemed that he could die.

And many friends who loved him, and who live,
Give thanks to him - his was the magic touch
That plucked them from the death he scorned so much,
And like a shepherd homed them. Do not grieve
If you should pass this way in after years?
His was a life that shone too bright for tears.

**Frank Ziegler**

## A DEDICATION

How can we praise the brave young men
Who flexed their new and untried wings
And flew, like eaglets, free and bold,
No fettered slaves or underlings?

How can we tell of loyal men
Who worked long hours upon the ground,
In drizzling cold or tropic heat,
To serve their crews in honour bound?

How can we laud the gentle girls
Who nursed them, fed them, mastered arts
Of radar, plotting, ground control
And tender care of engine parts?

How can we honour those who came,
Through hardship, danger, fear and pain,
From Europe's crushed and bleeding lands,
To spread their wings and fight again?

How can we show our gratitude
To those who, of their own accord,
Came from our far-flung Commonwealth
To help us wield our shining sword?

How can we thank the men who crossed
The great Atlantic, deep and wide,
And left their New World far behind,
To fight for freedom at our side?

A generation, selflessly,
Gave up the flower of its youth,
A sacrifice so quietly made
That we might live in peace and truth.

All tears were shed long years ago,
But memories last for all our days,
And so, with pride, we make our vow
To keep our faith with them always.

**Audrey Grealy (1989)**

## THE DAWN BATTLE ORDER

Anxious looking youths,

Expressing nervous grin,
Giving the thumbs up,
Climb into their aircraft.

Take off time 0500 hours,

Hello chaps, this is the skipper,
Belt up. ready for take off,
The plane zoomed into the red dawn sky.

Course navigator, 105 degrees magnetic,

The Dutch coast ahead,
Then on to Germany,
Change course 095 degrees magnetic Skipper.

The silver snaking Rhine,

Loomed on the starboard,
Black puffs of flak,
Greet the Bomber Boys into Germany.

Into the Valley of the Ruhr,

Roared the chariots of death,
Hello Skipper, Fighter, Fighter,
Port quarter down, coming in at 300ft,
Prepare to turn port, Go, Go, Go!

The rattle of guns,

The smell of cordite,
Sickening the nervous stomachs,
Of the crews.

Hello Skipper, this is the Rear Gunner

Attack, broken, attack broken,
Fighter, veered to starboard,
Commence run in course.

Navigator to Skipper, four minutes to target,

Take run in Bombaimer,
Bomb doors open,
Coming on green marker,
One degree error
We can miss target by one mile.

Twenty five seconds, twenty four,

Steady, steady Skipper, steady,
Left, left, steady,
Bombs gone.

Bomb doors closed,

Hello, gunners, keep eyes open for fighters.

The Lancaster leaps forward,

Relieved of it's burden,
Diving slithering,
Throttles slammed wide open.

A volcano is raging below,

With incendiaries and bombs,
Creating a battered city.
The flak is beginning to recede,
The ground defence have been beaten.

The rendezvous is reached.

The surviving bombers,
Turn course for home,
That was how it was done,
Young men with moral fibre,
Helped by science and skill,
And Esprit de corps and a prayer.

**Albert Weatherall (195 Sqdn)**

## CIVVY STREET

No more the red T.I.'s backed up by green.
No more the fear of fighters yet unseen.
For now each night we're home at six-fifteen!

Nor yet again the sickening corkscrew dive.
The miracle that we are still alive.
For now we're in the office nine to five.

No longer do we need to dodge the 'flak'.
Nor drink to those who won't be coming back.
For now our only fear will be the 'sack'.

**Jim Brookbank**

## AN IRISH AIRMAN FORSEES HIS DEATH

I know that I shall meet my fate
Somewhere among the clouds above;
Those that I fight I do not hate,
Those that I guard I do not love.

My country is Kiltartan Cross,
My countrymen Kiltartan's poor;
No likely end could bring them loss
Or leave them happier than before.

Nor law, nor duty bade me fight,
Nor public men, nor cheering crowds.
A lonely impulse of delight
Drove to this tumult in the clouds.

I balanced all, brought all to mind,
The years to come seemed waste of breath,
A waste of breath the years behind,
In balance with this life, this death.

**William Butler Yeats**

## I LOVE TO FLY A WHITLEY THREE

I love to fly a Whitley Three
In daylight over Germany,
And have the M.E.'s after me
It's foolish but it's fun!

There's bags of M.E. One-One-O's
And M.E. One-O-Nines,
And if you crash-land on the beach
There's always lots of mines

I love to fly a Whitley Five
And put her in a power dive,
And pull her out at One-nine-five,
It's foolish but it's fun.

I'd love to fly a Whitley Ten
I dunno where, I dunno when
And bomb old Hitler in his den
It's foolish but it's fun.

**51 Squadron (1941)**

## EIGHT LITTLE CYLINDERS

Eight little cylinders sitting facing heaven,
One blew its head off - then there were seven.
Seven little cylinders used to playing tricks,
One warped its inlet valve - then there were six.
Six little cylinders working all alive,
One got a sooted plug - then there were five.
Five little cylinders working all the more,
One over-worked itself - then there were four.
Four little cylinders flying o'er the sea,
One shed a piston ring - then there were three.
Three little cylinders wond'ring what to do,
One over-oiled itself - then there were two.
Two little cylinders very nearly done,
One broke a valve stem - then there was one.
One little cylinder trying to pull round seven,
At last gave its efforts up and ascended into heaven.

**Royal Flying Corps (1912)**

## PER ARDUA

They that have climbed the white mists of the morning,
They that have soared, before the world's awake,
To herald up their foemen to them, scorning
The thin dawn's rest their weary folk might take.

Some that have left other mouths to tell the story
Of high blue battle quite young limbs that bled.
How they had thundered up the clouds to glory,
Or fallen to an English field stained red.

Because my faltering feet would fail I find them
Laughing beside me, steadying the hand
That seeks their deadly courage yet behind them
The cold light dies in that once brilliant land.

Do these, who help the quickened pulse run slowly
Whose stern remembered image cools the brow
Till the far dawn of Victory know only
Night's darkness, and Valhalla's silence now?

**John Magee (1941)**

## THE UNPAYABLE DEBT

Willingly they answered the country's call,
Gave up their peace time living to fight for us all.
From cities and hamlets, fenlands and hills
From the Empire they came offering their skills.

Ground staff and aircrew they each played a part
In taking the war straight to the enemy's heart,
So many died that we might live in peace
That our unpayable debt can only increase.

Some decades later and older than their years
They returned to reflect and share silent tears,
Remembering when conflict filled the sky and the earth
And each of them proved to be more than his worth.

The unchanged winding lanes welcomed them back
To the nearby village church and a special plaque
Which in sombre metal on sacred stone
Acknowledges that debt for which we cannot atone.

**Joyce Lucas (Lincoln)**

## THOUGHTS AT A WAR GRAVE

Were thoughts in your mind on that very last flight,
That you'd never again see the morning's light?
Flying into hostile enemy terrain,
Never to see your homeland again.

Did death come fast or painfully slow?
Questions unanswered for we'll never know.
A stark telegram in a buff envelope,
Then long days of waiting hope against hope.

But hoping and praying were all in vain,
In foreign fields now your body is lain.
One of so many not of "The Few":
So many hundreds lie here with you.

A simple white stone with just name and number,
Here with your comrades in endless number.
We never said "Goodbye" and yet,
Your young shining face we'll never forget.

**Pat Gooding**

## THE GRAND OLD LADY

As I walked through the meadow I saw her,
Aloof with her nose in the air:
Ignoring the people who went passing by
Disdaining their curious stare.

Her legs, so delicate, seemed too frail
For the body they supported:
She had shared her life, with a great many men
Excitement and danger she courted.

But the days of her youth are now over
And it's true, she is well past her prime
'Just an old Lancaster bomber'
Once cherished by crews
That she brought safely back, every time.

**Ken Moore**

## TRIBUTE TO A LANCASTER

In one brief moment on a summer's day
You brought back memories of yesterday.
When you knew glory in those wartime skies,
But seemed outmoded in our children's eyes.
It won the war, I said to them with pride,
It's contributions cannot be denied.
Her crews were brave and dedicated men,
She flies as well as ever she did then.
Dear Lancaster, you great illustrious plane,
Wonderful to see you fly again.

**CWH Lancaster Support Club**

## A.C.2's ARE COMMON

A.C.2's are common,
A.C.1's are rare,
L.A.C's are plentiful,
You'll meet them anywhere.

Corporals they are stinkers,
Sergeants they are too.
But the Station Warrant Officer
Is a basket through and through.

**R.A.F. (Middle East 1936)**

## SECURITY

Empty your pockets, Tom, Dick and Harry,
Strip your identity, leave it behind.
Lawyer, garage-hand, grocer, don't tarry
With your own country, with your own kind.

Leave all your letters,suburb and township,
Green fen and grocery, slip-way and bay,
Hot spring and prairie, smoke stack and coal tip,
Leave in our keeping while you're away.

Tom, Dick and Harry, plain names and numbers,
Pilot, Observer and Gunner depart.
Their personal litter only encumbers
Somebody's head, somebody's heart.

**John Pudney**

## AIR RAID

I can remember well
The noise up in the sky
The urgency of sirens
To warn them passing by.

A dull and drowning noise
The sky was filled with awe
In every heart that walked the street
Lay fear to reach the house.

Safely in cellar
The bunker in the town,
Listening to the siren
It's over safely now.

Though somewhere in the land today
Another raid took place
Another row of houses
Send people to their graves.

The air was filled with thunder
The noise has disappeared
The morning sun broke through the clouds
And made the world at peace.

**Elisabeth Anna Marx (Gelsenkinchen, Germany)**

## AIRMAN'S PRAYER

God be with me up here above
I'm doing this for the ones I love
So that they may all stay free
To worship and have faith in Thee.

I do not want to hurt or kill
But if we don't the others will
So I have to do the things I do
That's why I'm in the Airforce blue.

And so dear God when I do these things
While flying up there on man made wings
Remember God, its' not my lust
I'm shooting them down because I must.

So that the ones at home stay free
And be just what they want to be
Please God, guide me in my flight -
I have to make day or night.

And when these flights have been done
And our victory has been won
Then we can leave Berlin and Rome
And head our ships for home sweet home.

**John Obee (1943)**

## BREAKFAST

His place was laid,
The messroom clock struck eight,
The sun shone through the window
On his chair.

No one commented on his fate,
Save for a headshake here and there;
Only old George, who'd seen him die
Spinning against the autumn sky,
Leaned forward and turned down his plate.

And, as he did , the sunlight fled,
As though the sky he'd loved so
Mourned her dead.

**Hannah M. Hunt. (1940)**

## AMEN

The first thing we'll pray for,
We'll pray for some beer,
Glorious, glorious, glorious beer!
If we only have one beer,
May we also have ten
May we have a blinking brewery!
Said the airmen, "Amen".

The next thing we'll pray for,
We'll pray for some girls,
Glorious, glorious, glorious girls!
If we only have one girl
May we also have ten,
May we have a blinking harem!
Said the airmen, "Amen".

The next thing we'll pray for,
We'll pray for the Queen,
The glorious, glorious, glorious Queen!
If she only has one son
May she also have ten,
May she have a blinking squadron!
Said the airmen, "Amen".

The last thing we'll pray for,
We'll pray for the erk,
The poor wretched blighter who does all the work!
If he only serves one year
May he also serve ten,
May he serve for blinking ever!
Said the airmen, "AMEN!".

**R.A.F Singapore (1930)**

## ODE TO A WOP/AG

No silver wings adorne his chest,
He leads no squadron into flight,
His job is to control the waves
That guides them safely through the night.

Not for him the front page news,
Nor does his face reflect the same,
An Op to him is just a cruise
A trip out there and back again.

**Author unknown - incomplete - Blackpool 1941 Ted Cachart**

## THE BALLARD OF A BRISTOL FIGHTER

There's a good half-dozen 'buses
On which I've done a whack,
From the R.E.8 to the three-ton weight
Of the lumbering old Big Ack.
On a rotary-engined Avro,
I've attempted several tricks
And I'm quite a dab at steering a Crab
(Better known as a D.H.6.).

And many a first-rate joy-ride
Have I had on 'em last and first,
And many a strut have I had go phut,
And many a wheel tyre burst.
But none of them know the secret
Of making my heart rejoice
Like a well-rigged Bristol Fighter
With a two-six-four Rolls Royce.

She leans at her place on the tarmac
Like a Tiger crouched for a spring,
From the arching spine of her fuselage line
To the ample spread of her wing.
With her tyres like sinews tautened
And her tail-skid's jaunty twist,
Her grey-cowled snout juts grimly out
Like a tight-clenched boxer's fist.

Is there a sweeter music,
A more contenting sound,
Than the purring clop of her broad-curved prop
As it gently ticks around?
Open her out crescendo
To a deep-toned swelling roar,
Till she quivers and rocks as she strains at the chocks
And clamours amain to soar.

Whisk 'em away, my hearties,
Taxi her into the wind,
Then away we skim on a spinning rim
With the tail well up behind;
Hold her down to a hundred,
Then up in a climbing turn
And off we sweep in a speckless sky
Till we catch our breath in the air Alp-high.
I wouldn't exchange my seat, not I,
For a thousand pounds to burn.

**H. T. Burt**

## THERE'S ALWAYS BLOODY SOMETHING!

Bloody times are bloody hard
Bloody wire for bloody guard
Bloody dogs in bloody yard
Bloody! Bloody! Bloody!

Bloody tea is bloody vile
Bloody coffee makes you smile
Cocoa made in bloody style
Bloody! Bloody! Bloody!

Bloody ice-rink's bloody mud
Bloody skates no bloody good
Sat where once I bloody stood
Bloody! Bloody! Bloody!

Bloody salmon's bloody queer
Looks at you with bloody leer
Is it good? No bloody fear
Bloody! Bloody! Bloody!

Bloody bridge all bloody day
Learning how to bloody play
Bloody backwards - anyway
Bloody! Bloody! Bloody!

Now and then the bloody stale
Censor hands out bloody mail
Better draw the bloody veil
Bloody! Bloody! Bloody!

Bloody girl-friend drops me flat
Like a dog on bloody mat
Gets a Yank like bloody that
Bloody! Bloody! Bloody!

Bloody sawdust in the bread
Must have come from bloody bed
Might as well be bloody dead
Bloody! Bloody! Bloody!

Bloody flies can bloody bite
Tickle all their bloody might
Always lose the bloody fight
Bloody! Bloody! Bloody!

Nearly reached the bloody end
Almost round the bloody bend
That's the general bloody trend
Bloody! Bloody! Bloody!

Don't it get your bloody goat
Was it Shaw who bloody wrote
'Where the hell's that bloody boat?'
Bloody! Bloody! Bloody!

**Sgt John Shaw**
**(Via Ted Cachart) - 1944 Stalag 357 Fallingbostel**

## BIRD-LIFE - THE LESSER HALF-BREVET

Come all ye men of tongue and pen
Who spend your nights and days,
By press or mike - just as you like,
The pilot's deeds to praise.
Publicity - it seems to me,
Should still find time to sing,
A song of love - in favour of
The Bird of the single wing.

Who mans the guns to keep the Huns
Off the back of the pilot's neck?
Who will twist and turn till his eyeballs burn
As he searches the sky for a speck?
Who'll first expose his unfortunate nose
To the Focke-Wulf's murderous sting?
Ask thc pilot hc'll tell you to see
The Bird of the single wing.

And who must know all his radio
From 'A' to the bitter 'Z' ?
Able to read what some clot has keyed
In a fit of insanity?
Who's got to crawl in a space so small
That a cat you could never swing?
This contortionist I present to you
Is the Bird of the single wing.

Who gets the girls with the heavenly curls
And the lips like a Cupid's bow?
And sings out "Ooh. You wonderful you,
How high do you really go?"
On who's manly chest does her little head rest
As his nose gets set for the ring?
On the pilot's of course - she'd have to use force
On the Bird of the single wing.

**N.Z. Air Gunner**

## BOMBER COUNTY

The skies are empty now as darkness falls,
The bare deserted runways scarred with weeds
Across the lonely fen a night bird calls,
The wind sighs softly in the whispering reeds.

A fitful moon rides through the cloudy blue,
A bomber's moon, remembered now no more,
Where once the very air vibrated to
The mighty Merlin engines' throbbing roar.

Dispersal huts stand crumbling and forlorn,
Their broken windows open to the rain,
The taxi track is fringed with waving corn,
The echoing hangars used for storing grain.

Upon the cracking tarmac wander sheep,
A derelict crew-room door creaks in the breeze,
The silent world around is lost in sleep
And stars are twinkling far above the trees.

Those very stars which were a friendly aid
To those who flew upon the wings of night,
The crews who never grudged the price they paid
To keep aglow the flame of freedom's right.

There is no flarepath now to show the way,
And guide the homing bombers to the ground
The old control tower stands in gaunt decay,
In silence and in darkness wrapped around.

Remember those who flew, across the years,
Those bright young lives they gave so long ago,
No looking back with bitterness or tears,
But thankfulness - for they would wish it so.

**Audrey Grealy**

## BOMBER'S MOON

'44 in Bomber County
Young men waiting for the night,
In the hedgerows birds are singing,
Singing in the falling light.
And the captain says, "Tonight there'll be a bomber's moon,
We'll be there and back underneath a bomber's moon".
A thousand bombers over the northern sea
Heading out, out for Germany.'

Chalkey White stands at the dartboard,
Curly Thompson writes to his wife,
Nobby Clarke and Jumbo Johnson
Are playing cards and smoking pipes,
And over the hangers rises a bomber's moon,
Full and clear rising, as the engines croon
And the planes they taxi out on to runway five
And sail off out into the silvery night.

Sandy Campbell checks his oil gauge,
The Belgian coast is coming soon;
Curly Thompson lifts his sextant,
Lines up on a bomber's moon
And waves are shining there beneath the bomber's moon.
The Lancasters flying high beneath the bomber's moon
Coming in along the Belgian coast
A thousand silver-shrouded ghosts.

Flak flies up around the city,
Jumbo Johnson banks the plane,
Goes in low and drops his payload,
Turns to join the pack again.
And people are dying there beneath the bomber's moon,
The city's a raging hell beneath the bomber's moon,
And the planes head out towards the northern sea:
Young men coming home from victory.

Over Belgium came the fighters,
Flying high against the night;
Curly Thompson saw them coming,
Closing in before he died.
And the young men shot them down beneath the bomber's moon,
Shot them down in flames beneath the bomber's moon;
Young men sending young men to their graves
Saw them down into the North Sea waves.

Now it's '44 in Bomber County
Mrs White dusts the picture and she cries:
Chalky White in uniform
Looking as he did the day he died.
And for God's sake no more bomber's moons,
No more young men going out to die too soon,
Old men sending young men out to die,
Young men dying for a politician's lie.

**Mike Harding (Stage T.V. & R**adio)

## CLIMB, WEAVE & SOAR

I'd watched them climb & weave & soar,
I'd heard that special engine roar
In those few weeks of '39
And longed that this may soon be mine.
'Til one day with indecent haste
A letter in my hand was placed,
An invitation - if that's the word -
'Twas now the time my loins to gird.

The ACRC buzzed and seethed
With those who lived & loved & breathed
That passion, to be part of course,
As aircrew of that great Air Force.
But what of weeks & months ahead
Of Footdrill, PT, Shooting, School;
Where would-be Flyers could only drool
To watch them climb & weave & soar,
And wonder what all this was for.

Yet suddenly the basics finished,
The spirits rose - still undiminished -
As Tiger Moths & Maggies too,
Presented, quite acceptably, a view
Which promised that the future could,
(Providing tests and marks were good,)
Give hope that not too far away
Must be that very Special day.

The day that was to be the best,
When 'Scrambled Egg' pinned Wings to chest,
Shook hands & smiled & said "Well Done",
"Good Luck - the job has now begun!"
With eager tread and early pride
Which none who passed felt need to hide,
Moved firmly through the open door
To join the climb & weave & soar.

And as the days and nights rolled by
So each their ordered duties flew
With mind and skills at his command
Gained by the early days demands
And thoughts which oftide still relied
On basics taught; and experience grew;
Youths became men, men became more
And graced the climb & weave & soar.

Some, nay many, through luck or chance,
Or just because it's meant that way,
Finished out the aerial dance
And fly those memories today.
The others, still masters of that sky
Chosen as their place to die,
Still dive & climb & weave & soar
To be remembered evermore.

So prize that sky, the clouds, the rain,
And with the Sun ... Thank them again.

**Flt/Lt Rex Chapple (1975)**

## THE D-DAY DODGERS

We're the D-Day Dodgers, out in Italy,
Drinking all the vino, always on the spree,
We didn't land with Eisenhower,
And so we fear we're just a shower,
'Cos we're the D-Day Dodgers in 'sunny' Italy.

We landed at Salerno, a holiday with pay,
Jerry turned his Air Force out, to cheer us on our way;
Showed us the sights and gave us tea,
We all got tight, the beer was free,
We are the D-Day Dodgers, way out in Italy.

Then we got the gen that we were going home,
Back to dear old Blighty, instead of into Rome,
But was it that? No, oh dear no!'
'Twas Naples first, then Anzio,
We are the D-Day Dodgers way out in Italy.

You've heard of Lady Astor, our pin-up girl out here,
She is the dear old lady who tried to stop our beer,
And when we get our Astor band,
We'll be the proudest in the land,
We are the D-Day Dodgers, way out in Italy.

Then they told us one day we might go to France,
There they said we'd have to fight instead of dine and dance,
But if we went to France we'd have to shine
You can't do that in a Spitfire Nine,
And we've never seen a Tempest out here in Italy.

**2nd T.A.F. (Italy)**

## COLOGNE 1942

The briefing room was crowded
With twenty crews, or more
We saw the target map and route
And guessed what was in store
The air is thick with rumour
"Its a Happy Valley treat"
The C.O. enters quickly
We clatter to our feet
"A message from the C-in-C"
We raise a muted groan
"A thousand aircraft on tonight
Your target is Cologne"
"A thousand aircraft" echoes round
A mocking cheer is raised
"Four hundred Tiger Moths" one quips
Yet still we are amazed
"Your job tonight - to start the fires
First there will find it tough
Make it easy for the heavies
To drop their back-room stuff"

"A thousand aircraft on Cologne
God help the bods below
With a full moon and a clear sky
God help the bods that go"
The banter crackles back and forth
Weak jokes that mask strong fears
For some, this night will end with death
With horror, grief and tears
And so we saunter to the flights
Each with his thoughts alone
Warsaw, Rotterdam, London burned
For them - tonight ....... Cologne.

**George Cocker**

## NOW I AM AN A.C.3

I joined the R.A.F. as an aircrafthand as good as good could be,
But after a month my Conduct Sheet was one of the sights to see;

It was full of fines and days in Quod my Leader gave to me,
I was five times up to the Wing Commo and twice to the A.O.C.
So I started again as an A.C.2, and now I'm an A.C.3.

**R.A.F. Cadet College. Cranwell. (1924)**

## THE DYING AVIATOR

A poor aviator lay dying,
At the end of a bright summer's day,
His comrades were gathered around him
To carry his fragments away.

He spat out a valve and a gasket
And stirred in the sump, where he lay,
And then to his wondering comrades
These brave parting words he did say:

Take the cylinders out of my kidneys,
The connecting rod out of my brain,
From the small of my back get the camshaft,
And assemble the engine again

Two valve springs you'll find in my stomach
Three spark plugs are safe in my lung,
The prop is in splinters inside me,
To my fingers the joystick has clung.

Take the prop boss out of my liver
The aileron out of my thigh,
From the seat of my pants take the pistons,
Then see if the old kite will fly.

Then get you two little white tombstones,
Put them one at my head and my toe
And get you a pen-knife and scratch there:
"Here lies a poor pilot below"

And get six brandies and sodas,
And set them all out in a row,
And get you six other good airmen
To drink to this pilot below.

And when, at the Court of Enquiry
They ask for the reason I died,
Please say I forgot "Twice Iota"
Is the minimum angle of glide.

Oh! had I the wings of an Avro,
Far away, into Holland I'd fly,
I'd stop there until the war's over
And laugh at you blighters on high

**Royal Flying Corps (1908)**

## THE CREW

**Pilot: (What He Says Goes: What He Does Counts)**

Who is the man up front, this Driver-Airframe?
Pilot? Captain? What's in a name
Let's say he's just another member of the crew
But this description simply will not do
He's trained to fly this kite, agreed,
But more, much more, he's there to lead:
To bring us back unscathed and sane,
Not once, but time and time again,
We looked to him for miracles of mind and will,
For deeds beyond the range of human skill:
What words of ours describe him well?
No words suffice: we called him 'Skip'
and followed him to Hell.

**Navigator: (To Guide You There and Back)**

Intent in his lamplit berth
He plies his precise trade
With dogged skill
His steady nerves and nimble brain
Manipulating the cyphers of his craft
Blind to the ground he covers
He brings us unerringly
To an exact rendezvous and home again,
Battling against darkness,
Contrary winds, fatigue, and the
Burden of our total trust.

**Bomb Aimer: (He Who Justifies the Means)**

His is the act that justifies
The journey:
The skill that deals the hammer blow
From base to target zone he
Plays small part,
But then, down in his cramped station,
Riveted to his bomb sight, prone,
Vulnerable, oblivious to all, except
the need to run up straight
and hit the mark, the stage is his:
The whole excuse for his existence
Concentrated in the brief pressure
Of an eager thumb.

**Wireless Operator: (A Good Listener and Vital as a Watch)**
Cocooned in a capsule of noise,
Straining his ears through static
For the frail thread of Morse,
He keeps his solitary listening watch,
Coaxing, with skilful fingers,
Strength into feeble signals.
Humoured as the dot-dash boffin
The eccentric key-basher, the fetch and carry merchant,
He soldiers on unappreciated until, one rough trip
Hit over the target, navigator half-dead,
Kite blown off course and pilot lost,
He brings them home on loop bearings
And fixes, to be known ever after
As the 'gen man'.

**Flight Engineer: (An Airborne Plumber-no Less)**
Of all of us, the engineer
Knew most about the aircraft gear:
Dials and switches, props and flaps
The drill if undercarts collapse.
What to do when fuses blow
Or overstressed components go:
Coping when hydraulics fail
Or bits fall off a damaged tail.
Oxygen, electrics, fuel,
Engines running hot or cool:
Something odd about the trim
All these queries came to him.
His duty, too, it was to share
His skipper's vigil in the air:
Providing one more pair of eyes
To scan the dark and dangerous skies.
A man of many parts who knew
His worth to pilot, plane and crew.

**Air Gunner: (Behind the Brownings' Bark)**
Alone in his transparent shell.
A speck in space,
He sits, poised in his airy kingdom:
At his back the unknown,
Before him the unfolding map
Of his journey,
Guardian of seven lives
Taut with the concentration of survival,
He swings his turret through vigilant arcs,
Eyes straining for the fighters,
Braced for the violence of surprise.

**Philip A Nicholson.**

## FAILED TO RETURN

Twilight in the autumn sky;
An airfield in the days of war.
The peaceful evening shattered by
The bomber squadron's engine roar.

Darkness over hostile land
Broken only by the light
Of probing tentacles that search
Unceasingly into the night.

Sinews of the bomber crew
Taughten as the light sweeps near,
Lest the beam detect their flight
And force them to acknowledge fear.

Moment of supreme relief,
The searching finger travels past.
Perspiration wiped from brow,
And prayers that the luck will last.

Flashes, crashes rend the sky:
The burst of anti-aircraft shell.
Blast and fragment that can turn
A moonless night into a hell.

The bomber throbs on endlessly
Toward its target far below.
The way ahead is lit by flames
That set the midnight sky aglow.

Concentration on the run-in.
Nothing can disturb their thought.
Searchlight, shell and conflagration,
All distractions to be fought.

"Bombs away!" Elated moment
As destruction hurtles down.
Bomb doors closed: evasive action:
Bomber crew is homeward bound.

Sharp staccato, bullets flying
As night fighters press attack.
Shells rip into bomber's framework.
Bomber's gunners firing back.

Blazing bomber badly crippled,
More staccato bullets flying.
Silence from the crippled bomber
With her gunners dead or dying.

What is left of crew abandon
Crashing bomber blazing bright.
Frantically escape hatch opens.
Airmen leap into the night.

Topsy turvy tumbling downwards,
Ripcord pulled to set things straight.
Parachute that billows open,
Slow descent and time to wait.

Down below the earth is waiting:
Some soft field to break the fall.
Dangling airman softly praying
No mishap will end it all.

All is blackness, then confusion,
Thud as airman meets the ground.
Canopy of parachute
Collapses as he looks around.

Straining ears are met by silence.
No one near to apprehend
The one who dropped down from the night sky.
No one near to act as friend.

Lonely airman, quite dejected;
Which direction should he roam?
Overhead companion bombers
Humming through the night for home.

Thoughts of England, home and loved ones:
Pity for them when they learn
He is one of many missing,
Wond'ring if he will return.

Sudden capture in the darkness:
Now to prison camp he goes.
Days of long interrogation:
Nobody about but foes.

Endless days and weary waiting:
Very little else to do.
So it ends, this final mission
Of a British bomber crew.

**Stan Fautley**

**THE ENGINEER'S FOLLY**

There was a young fellow who flew a Lanc,
And tended its engines with care.
He never was braggart and didn't pull rank,
And he loved a young WAAF who was fair.

Five objects he loved with a passionate pain,
And caressed ev'ry one with delight.
Not a day ever passed without kissing his Jane,
And he loved four Merlins at night.

Four props pulled his Lancaster into the air,
And dragged it to Berlin then home.
Where Jane waited patiently, doing her hair,
And working with brush and with comb.

His passion for Jane was a thing to behold,
Then he learned he had loved her too much.
So he worried all night in the altitudes cold,
And then began losing his touch.

He forgot to do this .. was too late doing that,
His Merlins they cried with neglect.
His mind was on one who would shortly be fat,
And a clothes line of nappies bedecked.

His instruments called him and begged for caresses,
But his mind wouldn't answer the call.
He thought only of her with the long golden tresses,
And how he'd encompassed her fall.

Came action that night with the fighters and flak,
With the Merlins required to excel.
But it soon became clear that they wouldn't get back,
And the crew would all finish in hell.

The engines protested, for they couldn't cope,
With the Engineer's folly that night.
And o'er the North Sea the crewmen lost hope,
As the Lancaster quickly lost height.

The moral dear reader is stick to one love,
Don't bring about her moral fall.
For whatever you find you are doing to her,
You'll quickly have done it to all.

**Roy Peters**

## PILOT'S HEAVEN

There's a place where good pilots go
Where they need no parachutes
Where the heavenly breezes blow
On their permanent flying suits.

They join the thrones up in the sky
Where the winged men finally meet
The men who were born to fly
And to go with their dreams complete.

For good pilots never die
They merely fly away
For they are happy in the sky
And it's there that they would stay.

If one should from the heavens fall
And crush out earthly things
Don't mourn, for after all,
He had feathered his permanent wings.

And now he roams the sky
In a ship sort, trim and true
Far too fast for human eyes
To see him in the blue.

**Lieut. J B MacArthur (USAAF)**

## THE FLIGHT MECHANIC'S SONG

Lords of the Air, they call us,
They voice our growing fame:
The front page of each paper
Adorned with a pilot's name.
In stories of deeds of valour
Inscribed up in the sky,
You read of high-speed battles
Fought by the men who fly.

There's one who gets no medals,
You never hear his name,
He does not fly in the pale blue sky
Nor pose for the News with a plane,
His job ain't called romantic
Or one for public gaze;
But the Lords of the Air respect him
And often give him praise.

**A Flight Mechanic (1942)**

## FRIEND OR FOE?

A Whitley in a dawning sky.
A shattered crew - some wounded,
Soon to die.
A long flog home.
A mucky job
Done best they could.
No golden strands of laughter now.
No flighty romance in the clouds.
A long flog home.

A Whitley in a dawning sky:
A thing heard droning, yet unseen.
Weary gunners wake and cry,
"There! There she blows!"
The long flog ended in a flash.
"Most likely fell near Grantham, that"

Said the gunner to his mate
"Another o' the Jerry's gorne! Well done!
I wonder what it was?"

**Christopher Deardon**

## FLIGHT LIEUTENANT

In the marsh the curlews cry
Beneath the empty bowl of sky,
Beneath the sun and flying cloud
Earth my grave and mud my shroud.
For forty years I've quietly lain
In the wreckage of my plane.

Baled out, they said, or Lost at Sea
But no-one came in search of me,
A distant ploughman drives his team,
And rushes rattle in the stream:
In summer time the cattle tread
Heavy-footed overhead.

Yet somehow in these bones I know
Man will devise machines that show
Where metal lies, and he will trace
My plane in its last resting place
Then will the lonely waiting cease
And these tired bones will rest at peace.

**K.D. Clarke**

## FOR YOU - DA VAR ISS OFER

When your tanks are gone and the course you're on
Promises a view of Dover
You get a surprise when you realise
For you "Da var iss ofer".

When that 'harmless' flak breaks your 24's back
No longer a skyway rover
As you're baling out, there is no doubt
For you "Da var iss ofer".

When you sight the Hun with his well aimed gun,
While his 'Kamerads' eagerly hover,
Around you they say, in their guttural way,
For you "Da var iss ofer".

As you march into town with an uneasy frown,
'Cos the guard had folks in Hanover,
You get the idea that starting right here
For you "Da var iss ofer".

When you become a Kriegie and are no longer free,
and you'd like to be a rover,
You wait for the day that they open the gate,
Then the G... D... war is over.

**Bill Dolgin (U.S.A.A.F Stalagluft 1 Barth 1944)**

## PAIN

I've joined the airforce!
He spoke with pride
His mother wept - his father sighed
Eighteen years old - a volunteer
Distant glory outshone his fear
His was the the joy of soaring flight
The ominous path of wings at night
His was a death in blazing hell
That burst and shattered as it fell
He didn't feel the slightest pain
The fighters bullets pierced his brain
It isn't he that I am sorry for
But his parents - they felt the pain of war.

**Unknown Volunteer**

## THE ERK'S LAMENT

Why did I join the R.A.F.?
Why can't I learn to fly?
Why can't I join this bloomin' war
And Spitfire in the sky?
Of flying we do nil all day,
Our duty's on the ground
Where even Squadron Leaders
Are terra firma bound.

Of stunting, jinking, we see none,
Of trips there's even less,
We spend our time in carting swill
And sweeping out the mess.
We're fitters, drivers, Woms and Wops,
Mechanics and G.D.'s,
We fill in forms and documents
And lubricate and grease.

The Warrant Officer is tough,
And Chiefy's even worse,
The Corporal carries all the cans,
The Police are one long curse.
Why did we join the R.A.F.?
Why can't we sweep the sky?
We're browned-off doing ground staff jobs-
Why can't we learn to fly?

**R.A.F Cranwell (1940)**

## FRED KARNO'S AIR CORPS

We are Fred Karno's Air Corps,
We are the R.F.C.,
We cannot fly,
We cannot shoot,
What ruddy use are we?
But when we get to Berlin
The Kaiser he will say,
"Hoch! Hoch! Mein Gott!
What a ruddy fine lot
Are the boys of the R.F.C.!"

**Royal Flying Corps (1915)**

## MY THANKS

When gazing at the skies, summer blue or midnight hue.
I picture airmen young and true, with laughing eyes.
With laughing eyes to hide the pain, of where they've been.
And how they've seen their good friends slain.
Expecting death on every raid, I hear the rumble of aircraft engines.
And feel so humble, at the sacrifices made!.

**Samantha Davis (Aged 11 years 1989)**

## FOR THE FALLEN

With proud thanks giving, a mother for her children,
England mourns for her dead across the sea.
Flesh of her flesh they were, spirit of her spirit,
Fallen in the cause of the free.

Solemn the drums thrill, death august and royal,
Sings sorrow up into immortal spheres,
There is music in the midst of desolation,
And a glory that shines upon our tears.

They went with songs to the battle, they were young,
Straight of limb, true of eye, steady and aglow.
They were staunch to the end against odds uncounted,
They fell with their faces to the foe.

They shall grow not old, as we that are left grow old,
Age shall not weary them, nor the years condemn.
At the going down of the sun, and in the morning,
We will remember them.

They mingle not with their laughing comrades again.
They sit no more at familiar tables of home,
They have no lot in our labour of the day time,
They sleep beyond England's foam.

But where our desires are, and our hopes profound,
Felt as a well spring that is hidden from sight,
To the innermost heart of their own, and they are known.
As the Stars are known to the night.

As the Stars that shall be bright when we are dust,
Moving in marches upon the heavenly plain,
As the Stars that are starry in the time of our darkness,
To the end, to the end they remain.

**Laurence Binyon (1869-1943)**

**FOUR OF THE BEST**

Engines turning, coughing, firing,
Unchained power rends the night.
Four propellers spinning faster,
Wings vibrating, poised for flight.

Engines racing, throttles open,
Tailplane rising, airborne now.
Fight to lift the heavy bomb-load,
"Come on! Climb! You sluggish cow!"

Engines throb in steady rhythm,
Target's over there, to port,
Keep your eyes peeled for the fighters
Hearts beat faster, nerves stretched taut.

Over target, flak is heavy,
Engines roaring - bomb-load gone.
Weave and turn to beat the searchlights
Get a course to head for home.

Flak has hit the starboard outer,
Engine races - shudders - dies.
Probing fingers of the searchlights
Hold the aircraft - blind the eyes.

Heading back across the Channel,
Starboard inner's running rough,
Fight to maintain height and urging
"Fly you Cow - Do your stuff!"

Engines shut down in dispersal,
Props turn slower . . . slower . . . stop.
In the silence - 'Bless those engines'
Safely through another Op'.

**Joe McLaughlin**

## THE GALLANT SIXTY-TWO

Oh they flapped and they panicked in the arid Arakan,
They were cut off and they knew, not what to do,
For the Japs had outmanoeuvred them (a very subtle plan)
So they had to go and call the Gallant Sixty-two.

We can fly them in, supply them in, or drop them from the tow,
Though the weather and the Jap may bid us nay,
They will be all right, by day or night, wherever they may go
For Sixty-two will always lead the way.

Then the Japs came a-prancing down the Manipuri Road,
And debouched into the narrow Imphal plain,
The Brown jobs were surrounded, and they found out they'd been joed,
Well, they had to call on Sixty-two again.

The Seventeenth from Tiddim - we sped their hasty way,
the Fifth to plug the Imphal Gap we flew,
And ne'er in Britain's history can anybody say
So much was done so quickly by so few.

Now Kabaw is a valley, 'Easy-Easy' a D.Z
Where the circuits, we admit, were rather wide,
Till the Jap one early morning thought he'd show his yellow head,
And shot two down by cutting round inside.

Through rain and cloud or anything you'll find us game,
Bumps and pockets, hills in mist are our delight.
This last we proved convincingly, with devastating aim
On the man who waved the flag upon Fort White.

The Fourteenth reached the Chindwin, they built a Bailey Bridge,
Which we 'shot up' very nicely every day,
Like flying fish we followed them, o'er every ruddy ridge,
And set them on the Road to Mandalay.

From Shwebo to Meiktila, Pyinmana to Rangoon,
The railways gave our aircrews quite a line,
And we'll fly by day and night and any bomber's moon.
Till Nippon's 'Rising Sun' sets in decline.

For it's lifts and drops and casualties, and men and mules and post,
Forever, till the Last Trumpet sound 'Review'
When St.Peter fights the Devil, and calls up the Holy Ghost,
He'll travel in a Dak from the Gallant Sixty-two.

**62 Sqdn (1944)**

## THE GUINEA PIG ANTHEM

We are McIndoe's army,
We are his Guinea Pigs.
With dermatomes and pedicles,
Glass eyes, false teeth and wigs.
And when we get our discharge
We'll shout with all our might:
"Per Ardua Ad Astra"
We'd rather drink than fight.

John Hunter runs the gas works,
Ross Tilley wields a knife.
And if they are not careful
They'll have your flaming life.
So, Guinea Pigs, stand steady
For all your surgeons' calls:
And if their hands aren't steady
They'll whip off both your (ears).

We've had some mad Australians,
Some French, some Czechs, some Poles;
We've even had some Yankees,
God bless their precious souls.
While as for the Canadians!
Ah! That's a different thing.
They couldn't stand our accent
And built a separate Wing.

**A Guinea Pig.**

## MY PRISON

And so another days creeps by
On the wall another mark
Twilight faded from the sky
My lonely cell grows dark.

A pale moon marks the evenings known
The hushed birds seek the nest
And my thoughts are turning home
To the ones I know the best.

Thus I mark another day
In the gloom I bow my head
And pray for loved ones far away
Then turn to my prison bed.

**Lieut. J. B. MacArthur (USAAF)**

## EPITAPH

Almighty and all present Power,
Short is the prayer I make to Thee;
I do not ask, in battle hour,
For any shield to cover me.
The vast unalterable way
From which the stars do not depart
May not be turned aside to stay
The bullet flying to my heart.

I ask no help to strike my foe,
I seek no petty victory here;
The enemy I hate, I know
To Thee, O God, is also dear.
But this I pray, be at my side
When death is drawing through the sky.
Almighty God, who also died,
Teach me the way that I should die.

**Hugh Rodwell Brodie (460 Sqdn R.A.A.F)**

## INITIATION

That I have lived to see men fly
In remote reaches of the sky,
Ready the darkest hour to dare
In the deep spaces of the air,
To take their station by the stars,
And to stand sentry at the bars
Of sunset; to excel in speed
The very vulture, to exceed
For height the hawk, for grace the gull,
Man's marks and limits to annul,
Till earth shrink to an island, hung
The heaven's other orbs among,
And the world but a shadow seems
Of unintelligible dreams,
Staggers my soul. Therefore I see,
As knit in one society,
Seers, saints and airmen; all who rise
To the pure place of the clear skies
And read, as in a mirror's face,
The hidden things of time and space.

**E. Vine Hall**

## THE GHOSTS OF THE EIGHTH ATTACK

When first the roar of a D.H.4.,
Came sounding over the plain,
The clan who flew were tried and true,
And sound of heart and brain,
Our Squadron then lost gallant men,
And well we have learned their lack;
And we'll drink a toast to each brave ghost,
The Ghosts of the Eighth Attack.

Kingsland turned to a spin and burned,
Rex and Gallagher died
In battle flame on the field of fame,
With Mitchell by their side,
From death unveiled they never quailed,
Or broke upon the rack,
But well we ken they fought like men,
The Ghosts of the Eighth Attack!

Dean and Bateman and Hollingsworth
Death garnered, thigh and thew,
And Captain Shea, with his Irish way,
Virgin and Hartmann too.
Robinson, Martin, Grodecki,
And Mackey, and Womack;
Brave hearts of gold that now lie cold,
The Ghosts of the Eighth Attack

And I sometimes think, when the night winds howl,
And never a ship is out,
That I hear the roar of a D.H.4.,
And the wail of wires in doubt;
And I think I see in a spectre ship
Spirits that must come back;
And I hail them then, who have died like men,
The Ghosts of the Eighth Attack!

**J. L. Hitchings**

## IF I MUST BE A GUNNER

If I must be a gunner,
Then please Lord grant me grace,
That I may leave this station
With a smile upon my face.

I wished to be a pilot,
And you along with me,
But if we all were pilots
Where would the Air Force be?

It takes guts to be a gunner
To sit out in the tail
When the Messerschmitts are coming
And the slugs begin to wail.

The pilot's just a chauffeur,
Its his job to fly the plane;
But its we who do the fighting,
Though we may not get the fame.

If we must all be gunners,
Then let us make this bet.
We'll be the best damn gunners
That left this station yet.

**Cpl. George Harding (R.C.A.F.)**

## MISSING

Less said the better.
The bill unpaid, the dead letter,
No roses at the end
Of Smith, my friend.

Last words don't matter.
For there are none to flatter.
Words will not fill the post
Of Smith, the ghost.

For Smith, our brother,
Only son of loving mother,
The ocean lifted, stirred,
Leaving no word.

**John Pudney**

## SEVEN UNKNOWN ENGLISH AIRMEN

'7 unbekannt englische Flieger'.
Inscribed on a wooden cross
In a small village near Aachen:
One crew of that night's bomber loss.

But the crew were well-known to each other.
After twenty operations they knew
Their close friendship had held them together.
The mark of a first-rate crew.

Geoff, Phil, Bob, Norman and Arthur.
Dave the Nav and Eric their Skip
Were the crew of Lancaster Oboe.
Their old kite now on its last 'trip'.

They took off from R.A.F. Warboys.
With a 'Cookie' and G.P's aboard:
Cologne's industrial heart was their target
As into the sunset they soared.

By the time they arrived at the target.
Pathfinders had marked the place well:
Below them a blazing inferno,
Was there anything left?, who could tell!.

'Bombs away' - 'Set course two nine zero for home Skip
Let's get the hell out of here!'
'Push the throttles through the gate', Flight'
'By cripes, that last one was near!'.

But their Lanc had been spotted on radar,
A blip on the cathode ray screen
Of a prowling German nightfighter
So close, it could almost be seen.

The Messerschmidt pilot was careful
And used all his knowledge and skill
To place his machine in position
In order to make a cert 'kill'.

Directly below the Lancaster-
In blindspot, as all aircrew know-
The 110 guns aiming upwards,
Made ready to deal the death blow.

A long burst from two lethal cannon
Into wing tanks, that's a vulnerable spot.
An explosion - total disintegration
Of aircraft and aircrew - the lot!.

Bits fell over a very wide area,
The villagers did what they could:
The remains they solemnly buried,
And erected a cross made of wood.

'7 unbekannt englische Flieger'.
Nothing else about them is known,
Except that seven young English airmen
Died together after bombing Cologne.

**Eddie Gadsby (Falfield)**

## HIGH FLIGHT

Oh! I have slipped the surly bonds of Earth
And danced the skies on laughter-silvered wings;
Sunward I've climbed, and joined the tumbling mirth
Of sun-split clouds-and done a hundred things
You have not dreamed of-wheeled and soared and swung
High in the sunlit silence. Hov'ring there,
I've chased the shouting wind along, and flung
My eager craft through footless halls of air.
Up, up the long, delirious burning blue
I've topped the wind-swept heights with easy grace,
Where never lark, or even eagle flew-
And, while with silent, lifting mind I've trod
The high untrespassed sanctity of space,
Put out my hand and touched the face of God.

**John Magee (1941)**

## HIGH IN THE VELVET MANTLE

High in the velvet mantle of the night,
Above, with just the moonlight on their wings.
The vastness of the Great & Endless Universe
Made them feel the presence of the King of Kings.
The nights seemed long, as endless as the sky,
Night after night, their nerves were tightly drawn,
And quietly they prayed He'd guide their homeward flight,
That they may live to see the beauty of the coming dawn.

**Jim Davis (1989)**

**(International Air Monument, Plymouth.)**

## HINTON'S HEROES

Way back in 1940
We were told to praise the "Few"
The men who in Spitfires
Claimed Jerry from the blue.

The wreckage of their victims
Proclaimed their victory
In Surrey, Sussex and in Kent
From London to the sea.

But now I give you others
Also worthy of your praise:
Not for them nights of intruding
Or offensive sweeping days.

For they live up at Hinton
Cut off from their kind
And spend their days in working
Knee-deep in mud and 'bind'.

Arising in the dead of night,
In billets scattered wide
They drape themselves in sodden blue
And draw on mud-caked hide.

They drag their protesting feet
To a breakfast, cold, of beans
And then to cold ablutions
And paperless latrines.

Mounting by the moon's soft light:
They congregate on high
And stand in open-ordered ranks
Before that eagle eye.

Potatoes, mashed and apricots
Are offered to each erk
A queue, of course, for coffee
Then back again to work.

Their labours now completed
They pause once more to eat
But having opened up their pie
Decide that life is sweet.

To Colready, to Newbottle
And yet to Charlton site
The hapless, earthbound creatures
Return to spend the night.

They'll win no George Medal
They have no African Star
Their only consolation is
The Banbury Cross and Bar.

**Sgt. Durndell (Hinton 1943)**

## FOR JOHNNY

Do not despair
For Johnny-head-in-air;
He sleeps as sound
As Johnny underground.

Fetch out no shroud
For Johnny-in-the-cloud;
And keep your tears
For him in after years.

Better by far
For Johnny-the-bright-star,
To keep your head,
And see his children fed.

**John Pudney**

## THE GUNNERS SONG

At night we fly to Hamburg
To Berlin or the Ruhr
Another trip another 'Op'
Will I ever end this tour?.

Another flare another fight
Another airman dies
The pungent air's our battlefield
Our blood has stained the skies.

And it was just three months ago
When I was young and green
While now they call us veterans
Though my age is just nineteen.

Still I'll just go on flying
I guess my turn has got to come
How long Oh Lord, How long.

**Victor Cavendish (83 Sqdn)**

## THE JOY OF FLYING

When heavy on my tired mind
The world, and worldly things, do weigh,
And some sweet solace I would find,
Into the sky I love to stray,
And, all alone, to wander round
In lone seclusion from the ground.

Ah! Then what solitude is mine-
From grovelling mankind aloof!
Their road is but a thin-drawn line;
Their busy house a scarce-seen roof
That little stain of red and brown
They boast about! - It is their town!

How small their petty quarrels seem!
Poor, crawling multitudes below;
Which, like the ants, in feverish stream
From place to place move to and fro!
Like ants they work; like ants they fight,
Assuming blindly they are right.

Soon their existence I forget,
In joy that on these flashing wings
I cleave the skies - Oh! let them fret
Now know I why the skylark sings
Untrammeled in the boundless air
For mine it is his bliss to share!

Now do I mount a billowy cloud,
Now do I sail o'er a hill,
And with a seagull's skill endowed
Circle, and wheel, and drop at will
Above the villages asleep,
Above the valleys, shadowed deep.

Above the water-meadows green
Whose streams, which intermingled flow
Like silver lattice-work are seen
Agleam upon the plain below
Above the woods, whose naked trees
Move new-born buds upon the breeze.

And far away above the haze
I see white mountain-summits rise
Whose snow with sunlight is ablaze
And shines against the distant skies.
Such thoughts these towering ranges bring
That I float on a-wondering!

So do I love to travel on
Through lonely skies, myself alone;
For then the feverish threat is gone
Which on this earth I oft have known.
Kind is the God who lets me fly
In sweet seclusion through the sky!

**Paul Bewsher D.S.C (R.N.A.S.)**

## JETS

And nature blossoms on, serenely oblivious
of the holocaust, the shivering grass
withstanding a man-made hurricane.
The shuddering earth trembles as the
Jet roars into life. A monster unleashed
with abbreviated wings and stunted body
spitting venom and power over the good earth.

Thrusting strongly, shattering the serenity
of a cloudless sky. Roaring into the horizon
pouring miles into the melting pot,
mocking a serene heaven.
A machine age monster challenging the elements.

And nature blossoms on, the feathered congregation
flexing wings unmolested, sitting out a vigil,
unhurried, unflurried.
The Jet roars defiance at the heavens
prizing open the oyster, endeavouring
to find the pearl.

**Claire Overy**

## EPILOGUE

My brief sweet life is over
My eyes no longer see
No Christmas Trees, no Summer walks
No pretty girls for me
I've got the chop, I've had it
My mighty Ops are done
Yet in another hundred years
I'll still be twenty one.

**R. W. Gilbert (Skellingthorpe)**

## LANCASTER TRIP

Red and Green markers burning bright,
Lead us through the murk of night.
Bomb doors open, running up for the drop,
Flak bursting too close, us trying to stop.

Searchlights sweeping in blue-white arc,
Hunting us, their prey in the dark.
Prop tips now blurred in a gleaming spin,
Chattering Brownings add to the din.

Steady now Skip., hold the run up straight,
Four seconds more and we lose the freight.
Bombs away and surge of upward lift,
Should drop true, compensated for drift.

Brilliant Chrysanthemums bloom far below,
Gold changing to red in a fiery glow.
Fountains of sparks climb into the night,
The Devil himself must welcome the sight.

Bomb doors closed, now turning for base,
Hoping Junkers will not give chase.
Course two-six-zero, the winds from the West,
With luck we'll make it, we've given our best.

Keep our height past Haarlem where fighters can rally,
The lights will illuminate all of Bomb Alley.
Revenge will be sought by Messerschmitt and Heinkel,
With Oerlikon and Spandau we've no wish to trifle.

Gunners keep watch from your perspex domes,
We're depending on you to see our homes.
Counter the cold by rubbing hands on your knees,
And be sure to see that the breech blocks don't freeze.

And when it's all downhill over the drink,
Don't kid yourself that the dinghy won't sink.
Watch fuel and oil pressure the whole of the time,
For Neptune awaits you when you think everything's fine.

With flarepath ahead, lead-in funnels alight,
Do not relax at such a welcoming sight.
For when you select the undercart down,
You could find that Jerry has made you a clown.

Hydraulics shot up, without flaps and wheels,
All oil has drained from those broken seals.
Belly flop on the grass, there's only one try,
Props tearing up turf and flinging it high.

The C.O. blasts you for wrecking the kite,
You must control yourself with all your might.
Think of England and all that you hold dear,
Then ask yourself, why did you volunteer?

**Len Hurle (1942)**

## LEST WE FORGET

One day a breed of men were born,
from every walk of life,
they came from near and far to fight,
for a certain way of life.

Some were tall and some were short,
and some were dark and lean,
and some spoke different languages,
but all were young and keen.

They all trained hard, and then one day,
a Wing Commander came
and pinned upon their breast, a badge,
Air-Gunners they became.

A squadron was their final goal,
to join an aircraft crew,
on Wimpeys, Lancs and Stirlings,
and some on Blenheims too.

They fought at night and in the day,
their op's increased in number,
some returned - and some did not,
for 'thirty' was the number.

Some survived to reach this mark,
and some continued flying,
some spent years behind the bars,
with many of them dying.

At last the victory came in sight,
the runways now are silent,
the echoes of the past remain
a conflict, long, and violent.

This breed of men are now but few
but they remember others,
who flew with them so long ago,
their Royal Air Force brothers.

**Bunny Austin**

## TO ANY MOTHER

Weep not, lady, though no more
He shall pass in by your door,
Though the garden gate is wide
And his footmarks scarce have dried,
Where he trod his merry way
On his last leave's final day!

So he went, as once he came,
Calling you by that dear name,
As a schoolboy back from class,
Buoyant as the clouds that pass-
He was like a schoolboy, then
Off to that harsh school of men!

Weep not, lady! Did you teach
What the parsons try to preach-
That a man's life only means
What the eager spirit gleans,
That at twenty he may see
What's still hid at eighty-three!

This he knew: it was no end
Suddenly to meet his Friend!
Suddenly to meet those others,
Those, his comrades - those, his brothers!
This is truth. This thing I know-
No such moment merits woe!

**Anthony Richardson**

## SHOWPIECE ... LANCASTER

I dream now of another time,
Of soaring wings and slipstream whine
Of airscrew arcs and engine drone,
And cloudy canyons I have known.

Once we were many, and we knew,
The love of thousands, our aircrew,
So many lovers, past recall,
Yet we were faithful to them all.

When towering columns split the night,
With brilliant beams of searching light,
Then in just moments we became,
Small insects. round a naked flame.

And with us then, our young men knew,
An eighth, unwanted, crewman flew,
He whispered, taunted, often near,
Unseen but known, for he was fear.

Time after time, we saw the cost,
To all who fought so well, yet lost,
For them a fiery plunge through space,
In another time, another place.

For you old lovers, youth has gone,
Relentless, time is moving on,
With arms outstretched, with measured pace
To take you all in cold embrace.

Time has not marred my grim old frame,
To your fading eyes, I am the same,
Look well, all strangers standing there,
For I'm the mighty LANCASTER.

**Walter Scott (630 Sqdn)**

**LANCASTER**

In the dark cold night
When we were warm in bed
The great big Lancaster
Flew overhead.

The huge black shadow
Roared through the night
Some would live
But some would die.

Those seven brave men
Who went to war
To give us freedom
For evermore.

And now we grow up
In a world so free
But remember
They went for you and me.

**Lindsay Ward (Aged 10 - 1990)**

## MY LADY LANCASTER

A beauteous comely maid was she,
Her lovely form a joy to see,
She came as swiftly as the night,
As graceful as a bird in flight.

Into the green years of our life,
Not sweetheart true nor loving wife,
But dark, mysterious, proud, unknown,
To cherish, love but never own.

Respectfully we learned to pay
Our tributes to her day by day,
And as our lives with hers entwined,
Our joys, our fears, our-inner mind.

Became a mutual living thing
To take upon our journeying,
She opened wide her arms to share
With us the perils of the air.

Her steadfast spirit, loyal and true,
Was with us always as we flew,
She never faltered, even though
She might be wounded, weak and slow.

We raise our glasses, drink a toast,
Remembering a very host
of things that time cannot transcend,
A gallant mistress, servant, friend,
We loved her to the very end,
My lady Lancaster.

**Audrey Grealy (1982)**

## THE A.C.2. COLONEL

"There goes Lawrence", whispered the corporal in my ear
And mouth agape I chose to halt, then turned to stare
The Mint man seen: he unaware, alone, But I so very near
Think now of Deraa, Tafileh, Damascus - would I'd been there!.

And where to now, Colonel?, I mumble to myself and humbly hint
Tho' rode not I your camel trains nor smote with Auda's horsemen
Yet this I own back here at home I made my house The Mint
Where to indeed, its men will sigh, so soon to rest at Moreton.

**Sgt. W.J.Kindell. (M.T. Section 1928 - 1945)**

## LIE IN THE DARK AND LISTEN

Lie in the dark and listen,
It's clear tonight so the're flying high;
Hundreds of them, thousands perhaps?
Riding the icy, moonlight sky;
Men, material, bombs and maps,
Altimeters and guns and charts,
Coffee, sandwiches, fleece lined boots,
Bones and muscles and minds and hearts,
English saplings with English roots
Deep in the earth they've left below.
Lie in the dark and let them go.
Lie in the dark and listen.

Lie in the dark and listen,
They're going over in waves and waves,
High above villages, hills and streams,
Country churches and little graves,
And little citizen's worried dreams,
Very soon they'll have reached the sea
And far below them will lie the bays
And cliffs and coves and sands
Where they used to go for summer holidays.
Lie in the dark and let them go,
Their's is a world we'll never know,
Lie in the dark and listen.

Lie in the dark and listen,
City Magnates and steel contractors,
Factory workers and politicians,
Soft hysterical little actors,
Ballet dancers, reserved musicians,
Safe in your warm civilian bed,
Count your profit and count your sheep,
Life is passing above your head,
Just turn over and try to sleep.
Lie in the dark and let them go,
There's one debt you'll forever owe.
Lie in the dark and listen.

**Sir Noel Coward (1944)**

## ECHOES OF THE PAST

Like graceful birds across the sky,
Flashing silver as they fly,
There they go the people cry,
"SPITFIRES!"

Winging in an endless flight,
keeping guard by day and night,
Swooping low or gaining height.
"Our Fighters".

Battle of Britain waged and won,
Valiant men, their duty done,
This above all, and second to none,
"Our Pilots".

Heroes all, so brave and true,
Eternal thanks are due to you,
We all owe so much to "the Few",
In Hurricanes, Spitfires, mechanics and crew -
We salute you.

**Dorothy M. Loughran**

## OH! MARY THIS WAAF

Oh! Mary, this Waaf is a wonderful life,
Sure, you might get a job as an officer's wife.
There are plenty of airwomen just digging for gold,
At least, when I asked 'em, it's what I was told,
So I soon took a hand in this digging ye ken,
And I tried very hard to attract all the men,
Saluted quite smartly by winking one eye,
And ignored all the airmen unless they could fly.

A young Flight Lieutenant was the cause of my fall
So handsome, attractive, and heavenly tall,
Took me for a ride in his little M.G.,
When something went wrong with the engine, y'see.
We were running on Pool and 100 octane,
Though I shouted quite loudly, no help could obtain,
He'd twenty E.A.'s to his credit already,
So one little Waaf couldn't make him unsteady.

And now on my story I will not enlarge,
Sufficient to say that I got my discharge!

**The Waafery (1940)**

## SPICK AND SPAN

Said Sergeant Spick to Corporal Span
"Come 'ere, you 'orrid little man.
Well, ain't you changed them engines yet?
Bin scivin', playin' cards, I'll bet!".

Said Corporal Span to Sergeant Spick,
"I've done all four, Sarge - Pretty slick!
It wasn't easy on me tod
Workin' out that airframe mod."

Then Sergeant Spick, when once he'd seen,
Went red, then white, then pale green.
He frothed a bit, his voice grew skimpy
-"Mine God! Four Merlins in a Wimpey!".

"Come 'ere, you 'orrid little man ....."

**Christopher Dearden**

## THE PILOT CAN'T SWIM

They say in the RAF that a landing's OK.,
If the pilot can get up and still walk away,
But in the Fleet Air Arm the prospect is grim,
You look such a clot when the pilot can't swim.

If you come o'er the round-down and you see Wings frown,
You can safely assume that your hook isn't down,
A great big barrier looms up on high,
You hear Wings shout "Cut your engine, or die".

I thought I was coming in low enough,
But I was fifty feet up when the batsman gave "Cut",
Loud in my ears the sweet angels sang,
Float, float, you Pilot, you'll certainly prang.

They gave me a Seafire to beat up the Fleet,
I beat up the Rodney and Nelson a treat,
But forgot the high mast that sticks up from Formid,
And a seat in the 'Goofers' was worth fifty quid.

**Fleet Air Arm (1939)**

## IT WILL NEVER HAPPEN TO ME

"I'll always come back" said air-gunner Jack,
"That's one thing I'll put my shirt on.
I feel quite safe sitting alone at the back,
Its not I who'll go for a Burton"
But the Messerschmitt pilot had not heard this said
As he lined up his sights on the Lanc,
And Jack felt his parachute canopy spread,
As down in the darkness he sank.

"They'll never get me" said the young WOP/AG,
To the rest of the boys in the flight,
"Twenty Ops don't you see - Lady Luck flies with me,
She's with me by day and by night.
My Mickey-Mouse charm keeps me clear of all harm,
Friendly fortune takes care of our Bill"
But his luck went awry one night in the sky,
Through the shells of an eighty-eight mil.

"Of course I feel fear when the flacks very near",
Said Sam who had guns in the front.
"When the moonshine is brighter, the heavens are lighter
And the fighters are out on the hunt.
But my totem-pin wards me, my talisman guards me,
I trust and believe I'll come through"
But the flak came the wrong way and blew up the bomb-bay,
And Sam's gone to stay with his crew.

"I do not see why it just seems they all buy it"
Bert said to me up in the bar.
They're efficient and plucky - I guess we've been lucky,
We've each got a good guiding star.
We go off on ops, pull out all the stops,
Our good fortune ne'er seems to flag"
Now we're walking the wire - with less of our fire,
Together still - inside the bag!.

**Bill Rainford**

## NEVER GO BACK - THEY SAY

I went back to the old field
At the close of an Autumn day.
To find the tower crumbling,
The hangars filled with hay.

The dead leaves swirled and eddied
And crunched beneath my foot.
This concrete base, complete with plough,
Was once the gunners' hut.

What could it be, what was it
That I had come to find?
Traces of my vanished youth?
Or was it peace of mind?

The shadows darkened, lengthened,
As I slowly strolled around,
Stood and looked and listened
As they crept along the ground.

And then I heard - or did I?
A faintly mocking laugh,
The tinkle of a spanner,
The chuckle of a WAAF.

The muted sound of Merlins,
Throttles eased by ghostly hands,
Screech of tyres on tarmac,
The lost coming in to land.

For here were ghosts in plenty,
Young ghosts of yesteryear,
But I am young no longer
And am not wanted here.

I went back to the old field
At the close of an Autumn day.
I wish to God I'd listened,
And I had stayed away.

**Roy Collins (90 Sqdn)**

## LOST

"We're lost!" the navigator wailed
"I knew ? we never ought
To see the Rhine to starboard and
The House of Lords to port".

"I've, got it!" cried the engineer
(He'd caught it year's ago)
"It's all to do with Einstein
And the tides at Scapa Flow".

The navigator blew his stack
And bellowed acrid smoke,
Then wrote a letter to The Times,
And then his pencil broke.

At which the skipper got quite cross
And wished he hadn't joined
(But decency forbids to tell
The pungent words he coined).

"Well, point t'thing at Lincolnshire",
The gunner said at last.
"Tha'd better get a move on, lad,
That's Cairo we've just past!".

"I knew a girl in Cairo, once!"
The perky 'sparks' remarked.
So thrilling was the memory
He promptly disembarked.

"If I divide by ninety-nine",
The navigator mused,
"Then integrate reciprocals
We'll get the Hun confused".

"Look, never mind the bloody Hun",
The skipper snapped in haste.
"It's clear to me we're late for tea
My favourite, bloater paste".

And then he started singing in
A manner loud and wild
Behaviour which, the gunner thought,
Would scarce become a child.

Yet on they flew and ever on
With nothing on the clock.
"At this rate", moaned the engineer,
"We'll all end up in hock!".

But then the navigator grinned,
"I've worked it out, my son!
I think ? the answer is", he said,
"I think it can't be done!".

So, if you meet a Halifax
A-circling in space,
Don't be alarmed, it's just our lads
Still looking for their base.

**Christopher Deardon**

## A MAIDEN YOUNG AND FAIR.

A maiden young and fair was she
Brought up in high society
An airman young and bold was he
Who brought this maiden to despair.

Now when her apron strings would meet
He'd walk with her through snow and sleet
But when those strings they would not meet
He'd pass her by out in the street.

Her father, coming home one night,
Found his house without a light
He went upstairs to go to bed,
When suddenly he turned his head.

He went into his daughter's room
And found her hanging by a rope
He took his knife and cut her down,
And on her breast he found this note:

"I wish my baby had been born
Before these troubles had begun,
So dig my grave both wide and deep
And lay white lilies at my feet".

Now all you airmen bear in mind
A girl's true love is hard to find,
So if you find one good and true,
Don't change the old love for the new!.

**Author Unknown (1933)**

## NIL CARBORUNDUM

You'd wangled a forty-eighter
To meet up with your new son, Fred
Lord knows when there'd be another
'Cos the squadron was off to the Med!.

You'd sadly said your fond farewells
And left your poor wife in tears,
Then near the station the siren went
So you'd stopped for a few more beers.

You'd fully intended to ring the camp
Though it was a bit of a bind,
But when that H.E. put out the lights
It put that out of your mind.

You'd finally staggered through the gates
No kitbag and more than a singe
And you'd have thought you'd purposely
Gone AWOL just to have a binge'

They whipped you into the Guardroom,
Your feet scarcely touched the ground.
And it was "quiet you, that man there!"
Though you'd not even made a sound.

They soon had you down on a charge
Though it sounded a trivial offence,
Namely 'losing one RAF Kitbag'
But somehow that hardly made sense.

Although it was supposed to be mine
Now here's a ridiculous thing
It didn't really belong to me,
Being the property of H.M. the King.

And I didn't really lose it
It was blasted right out of my hand,
But in the Forces you didn't argue,
Left the talk to those in command.

So there I was in jankers,
Lonesome and all forlorn, browned off
And chocka and all sorts of things
Cursing the day I'd been born!.

And then I thought of a saying
I often used to think of then.
'Nil Carborundum'. which means-
To give you the Pukka Gen.

Don't let the so and so's grind you down,
Don't let them get under your skin!'
So I didn't then and I don't do now
'Cos it's the only way you can win!

**Joyce Lucas (Lincoln)**

## NO WEEPING NOW

I went back to the lonely Wolds,
The fens and the empty sky.
I saw the tall gaunt elms, heard the calling rooks,
How time had passed me by.

Grass had grown on the runways,
In the hangers stood rusting ploughs;
The dispersal points were empty,
Just starlings and grazing cows.

The Watch Office stood deserted.
Or maybe the ghosts of men:
Stood and watched as I walked remembering,
For I'd said I'll come back again.

The windsock hung in tatters,
Forlorn in the cold damp air,
Then I thought, 'What does it matter?,
There is nobody there to care.

The crew huts were but ruins,
Rotting timbers and sagging floors;
Not a voice to break the silence,
Just the wind and the creaking doors.

Then I recalled these once were billets,
Full of life and the noise of men:
With the crackling roar of Merlins,
Or the whispering scratch of a pen.

So I stood quite still to listen;
Was there a message there for me?
In the shadows would they remember,
Had they left me a sign to see?

If they had it was too elusive,
Made dim by the veil of years;
And I recalled all the purpose and courage,
Till my eyes were blurred by tears.

**J.R. Walsh (1976)**

## MAXIMUM EFFORT

My Airforce days were often bright and gay
But there were days of sadness and dismay
I'd get to know the crews that used the Mess
And get involved with some I must confess
I'd say farewell to some familiar face
But sometimes they would not return to Base
They'd take off in the prime of life to do
A job which would beat folk like me and you.

Young boys cut down in the prime of life
Some hadn't had the time to take a wife
Their attitude to life was to survive
Some of them managed to stay alive
They'd take off on another bombing raid
Some wouldn't even get back to be paid
They'd have to face another night of hell
Terror would sometimes hold them in it's spell.

I've seen them as their tour was near it's end
At breaking point, unable to unbend
The parties in the mess when their tour was done
But some were even too tired to have fun
They'd go on leave and not return to us
New crews would take their place without a fuss
They too would learn to see the Cathedral light
As a friend burning a welcome in the night
As they returned to Base, a job well done
Not everyone's idea of a night of fun.

I wonder what they think when they look back;
The crews that beat the searchlights and the flak
Do they think of the maximum effort they once gave
And of old friends forced into an early grave
They must wonder if their efforts were in vain
The world hell bent on conflict once again
Comradeship felt on an Airforce Base
Is something civilian life cannot replace
The ground crews and the aircrews joined as one
A maximum effort - A job well done.

**Peggy Clayton (Sgt WAAF)**

## THE IMMORTAL FEW

To eagles fallen. the glorious. the brave.
In a tidy churchyard or some unknown grave.
But memories are for veterans with their earthly toil.
Cold clay their reward in our rich warm soil.

Back to an era nigh on fifty years.
Life was for the living as they diced with their fears.
And signed their honour in a clear blue sky.
A heritage of pride, to fight and to die.

Each to their fate their Kismet had led.
On some foreign field their life force bled.
Just everyday "Boys", every mother's son.
Who loved and laughed then climbed into the sun.

Deed us the honour to accept their gift.
The wind neath our wings to Heaven will lift.
To meet those "Boys" in a dimension unknown.
Those silent Heroes with whom you have flown.

Those Knights of the air who received their call.
To face the enemy and to give their all.
They left us a legacy through the barriers of time.
To transcend this life to immortality sublime.

To those young warriors who've seen the Lord's face.
The victory is yours to receive now his grace.
To consummate their destiny, they've paid their earthly due.
And remain throughout Eternity, as the valiant Immortal Few.

**Jock Turner (RNZAF)**

## A GOLDEN STAR FOR A SOPWITH

Oh Mother put up your Golden Star,
Your son's gone up in a Sop.
The wings are weak, the ship's a freak,
It's got a rickety prop;
The motor's junk, your son is drunk,
He's sure to take a flop,
Oh, Mother, put up your Golden Star,
Your son's gone up in a Sop.

**A.A.F. 148 Sqdn (1917)**

## O RULER OF THE EARTH AND SKY

O Ruler of the earth and sky,
Be with our airmen when they fly:
And keep them in thy loving care
Amid the perils of the air.
O let our cry come unto thee
For those who fly o'er land and sea.

Strong son of man, save those who fly
Swift-winged across the uncharted sky;
Each anxious hour and lonely flight
Serenely unchallenged, day and night,
O'er land and ocean safely bear
All those in peril in the air.

O holy spirit, God's own power
Give peace in sudden dangers hour:
Bring calm of heart and be thou near
To those who watch, and those who fear,
To thee will rise the grateful prayer
Of those who serve thee in the air.

O trinity of love and grace
True guide of all who fly through space
In peace or war, 'mid friend or foe;
Be with them wheresoe'er they go.
So shall our praise with heavens blend
And joyful hearts to thee ascend.

**Hymn - "Eternal Father Strong To Save"**

## OF DAYS SO LONG AGO

When the night is still...
And the Moon is clear
The ghosts of the past are here
Of men long dead and machines sped
Into the valley of fear.

Of men who fought to save this land
From the onslaught of a power regime
Of pilots and Navs and Gunners and Sparks
Each one was one of the team.

Each one knew - that he had to do
His job as well he might
Each said a prayer - and some perished there
In the darkness of the night.

Dark shapes may rumble across the field
From a war that was fought and won
For these are the ghosts of aircraft and men
Whose landings will never come.

So when you cross this field again
Please think for a minute or so
Of those machines and of the men -
Of days so long ago.

**Peter Markham**

## THE OLD AIRFIELD

Where are those young men who slept within my walls,
Most are in lands beyond the seas.
They do not hear me cry out with pain
As the walls that kept them safe from wind and rain
Now neglected, begin to fall.

My watchtower stands,
Although its windows are broken and bent.
No more will young women climb those stairs
Or listen with headphones to the voice of a loved one
Returning from a raid and, for those who did not return,
Have a little cry.

No more as summer breezes blow
Will I smell the fragrance of their scent.
My operation block is just a shell;
The roof and doors are gone
But on summer nights when all is still,
Men of the phantom fleet return,
Hoping to meet a friend
For they have a story to tell.

My windsock and hangars stand tattered and torn,
Only the rooks around them fly,
Screaming out their mocking scorn.
My runways are all cracked with age,
Covered with weeds and debris too.
Those same runways from where mighty bombers flew,
Oh, "Where are all my young men, and women too".

**Cliff Sims**

## OUTWARD BOUND

A lightless ship on darkened danger,
Throbbing across an ocean far.
An ocean filled with the wrath of nature,
An ocean chilled with thoughts of War.

'Neath the Line engines thumped loud,
Men were awork there - heated - grimed.
Down 'neath the main deck, sleeping sound,
Youth of the nation - service men - primed.

Way up aloft a heavens companion,
Back to the stern - Gunners land.
Far to the for'ard the Captain's bastion,
There at the wheel a steady hand.

Lo' Eastward the day is dawning,
Soon the sun is there arrayed.
Gone the fears of night and morning,
Born the hope and calm of day.

Another world of sky and sea,
A drunk horizon far between.
The clouds unfurled at last are free,
To jaunt the air to land unseen.

The greying shadows grow far longer,
The tireless sun prepares to go.
Three men watch the passing wonder,
Three friends hum a tune you know.

A tune recalling days of leisure,
A smiling face - a "hello" there.
Small things making life a pleasure,
A cup of tea - a cosy chair.

Reality fades before their eyes,
Time and space are turned aside.
To each a cherished scene there lies,
Quickly feast - for such dainties die.

Perhaps a maid in chosen dress,
A struggling first, in a heated race;
The envied peace with men at chess;
A seasoned pipe 'side a fireplace.

A crowded dance floor - ankles near,
A medley of handshakes - smiles abound.
A furious band tapping modern cheer,
The grinning face of a lost friend found.

A sudden start as visions blur,
Sightless eyes blink, then gaze around.
Backs are turned on things that were;
They walk away - the sun is down.

**Charles Chillingworth (South Africa)**

## OPS

A biting wind, a searing frost,
A dome of cloud, a misty moon,
Below, a flaming holocaust,
The engines' heavy droning tune.

The spiteful deadly beads of flak
That weave a pattern on the night,
The searchlight cones across the black,
A piercing, vicious blinding white.

The aircraft jinking as it tries
To keep its course and yet evade
The fighters, swarming thick as flies,
That try to stem this cavalcade.

This endless wave, this marathon
Of vengeful bombers, dim and black,
Their crews, relentless, pressing on
To seek, to find and to attack.

A burning bomber hurtling down,
A blazing pyre across the sky,
The incandescence of a town
Alight with flares, prepared to die.

A voice upon the intercom,
The sudden chattering of a gun,
The fire-burst of a fallen bomb,
Its journey made, its duty done.

**Audrey Grealy (1982)**

## THE PILOT'S PSALM

The B.E. 2c is my bus, therefore shall I want,
It maketh me to come down in green pastures
It leadeth me where I would not go
It maketh me sick

It taketh me astray on all cross-country flights
Yea, though I fly o'er No-man's Land where mine
Enemies compass me about, I fear much evil,
For thou art with me; thy joystick and thy prop discomfort me.

Thou preparest a crash before me in the presence of mine enemies,
Thy V-8 anointeth my head with oil; thy tank leaketh badly.
Surely to goodness thou shalt not follow me all the days of my life,
Else I shall dwell in the House of Farnborough for ever.

**Royal Flying Corps (1916)**

## THE PARACHUTE PACKER'S PRAYER

When they posted me here to the section,
I was free as the pitiless air,
Unashamed of confessed imperfection,
Having no sort of burden to bear.
I was not an incurable slacker;
Neat, not fussy - I fancied of old,
But today I'm a Parachute Packer,
And my heart takes a turn with each fold.

When I think how I snugly resided
In the lap of this land we could lose,
I believe if I left one cord twisted,
I would place my own neck in a noose.
So I lay the fine silk on the table
And I lift each pale panel in turn.
They have said that my folding is able
But it took me a long time to learn.

For the cords must come free for smooth flowing
And the webbing attachment be stout,
For the brute of a breeze will be blowing
If the aircrew have to bale out.
'Cos the flyer must float unencumbered,
Come to earth to complete the design,
See, the 'chute has been carefully numbered,
And the name in the log book is mine.

So is conscience awakened and care born
In the heart of a negligent maid.
Fickle Aeolus, fight for the airborne,
Whom I strive with frail fingers to aid.
Give my heroes kind wind and fair weather,
Let no parachute sidle or slump,
For today we go warring together
And my soul will be there at the jump.

**G D Martineau**

## PASSING OF A HURRICANE

As I walked down by Lewis Lane
To buy a roasting duck
There passed a broken Hurricane
Dismembered on a truck.

Her wings lay folded at her side,
A blackened, tattered pall,
And gaping bullet-holes supplied
The context of her fall.

The canvas discs which normally
Screen the eight gun-vents' blast
Were shot away - brave proof that she
Fell firing to the last.

She went, and as I sort my roast
I thanked her for the day
When high above the Kentish coast
She dived into the fray.

And quite alone, no friends to see
Fought twenty Messerschmitts
Who, having scored but one to three,
Repented of their blitz.

Then sudden, as I stopped and stood,
A roar came deep and strong-
A squadron of her sisterhood
Throating their battlesong.

**"Ariel"**

## A PAY CLERK'S PLEA

Here is our little tale of woe
Some facts we think you ought to know.
How on a sweltering summer's day
We slave away to coin your pay.

And how in winter's coldest hour
With fingers numb and faces sour
We tell you your account's in debt
You say hard things we can't forget.

From eight o'clock till five at night
The aircrew take a great delight
In calling for a 'casual' - lying
Saying they've been out night flying.

The ground staff boys are not so bad.
But we find their greatest fad
Is just to phone us every minute
Ask for 'credits' - its the limit.

And if at times we should relax
Some airman queries income tax
And when at intervals quite rare
We slink away to comb our hair.

We are the weary workers then
Who fight the battle with the pen
We oft are told we'll cause this war
To last for ten long years or more.

Oh, isn't it a crying shame
That we should have to take the blame
And can you wonder we get flustered
Our only hope is to get remustered.

**Sgt. D. Bayley (WAAF 1943)**

## PETROL TINS GALORE

The Nissen hut's foundation
Is petrol tins galore
They are the one salvation
Of troops on Iceland's shore.
One tin to shave your face in,
One tin to brew your tea,
One tin is your washbasin,
One tin your lavatory.

One tin to mark the miles with
Along that ropey road,
And tins to put your files in
In cypher or in code,
One tin is for a shelter
To guard you in a raid,
And at the Mentaskollin,
Ten tins to store the braid.

One tin to warm your feet in,
And one to shade the light,
One tin to put your seat in,
And one to house a Flight
And lastly there's one tin
We'd like, (there'd be none better)
Packed full of lovely popsies
From the Windmill Theatre.

**Pascoe Thornton (1941)**

## THE SPROG

There's blood on the oil piping,
There's blood on the spar,
You blundering fairy
How stupid you are!
Oh, come on - get organized -
Pump some more juice,
And watch your rubber mask
Doesn't work loose!
Don't kick the control wires
Crumbs - switch off your 'mike',
When we're back on the 'deck'
You can play how you like!
You've pumped too much oil now
And fused the wrong flare,
While over the target
You just lie and stare!
Dear Lord above - help us
With 'rodded' stuff on
You'll press the wrong switch
Then we'll all get a 'gong',
But we won't live to wear it
With you still aboard
So you'd better bale out Joe
And pull the old cord!

**George Henfrey (1943)**

## THE PHANTOM OBSERVER

I watched their calm and quiet wait
As nightfall beckoned their coming fate.
I watched them when they took to wing
With flashing smile and thumbs-up grin.

I watched their stunning youth cut short
"Press on" they cried "We can't abort,
For who will end this bloody war?
Our lives are pledged - we can't do more".

I watched them brave the flames of Hell
I watched their pain as wingmates fell.
I watched them plunge their way to doom,
A flaming Lanc - their final tomb.

Who were these men I watched with care?
They saw me not but I was there.
Brave simple chaps who knew stark fear,
"The Salt of the Earth", I call them here.

I watch them yet in silent prayer,
Fond memories live - they still lie there,
For now I watch my grandchild play,
And thanks to them, I live today.

My watch must end, for years grow late.
And I, like them, do calmly wait
To join the gallant band in Heaven,
And serve once more with Number Seven.

**Ignatius McCann (1945)**

## DEAR GOD

In this busy turmoil'd world,
Your eyes are everywhere;
But there is one for whom I'm offering
This very special prayer.

If he should travel, once again,
To lands across the sea;
Make sure that he gets safely tbere-
Will you do this for me?

And when he finally arrives,
Is it too much to ask
For you to watch his every move,
His every little task?

And when he's up amongst the clouds
He'll be so near, that You
Won't have far to go, to see
That he comes smiling through.

Watch over each and every man-
The crew - of which he's part,
Please see that they return to base
Exactly as they start.

No matter where this boy should go,
Please bless his path of strife;
And please, dear Lord, watch over him,
And spare his youthful life.
AMEN

**Lynne Pickard (Canada 1941)**

## Q FOR GLORY

We waited until morning and her light
Bade farewell to the sombreness of night.
We waited vainly, hoping and praying,
Listening for a sound, the sound betraying
The presence of aircraft ... a faint hissing ..
But "One of our aircraft was missing".

How often we had waited in the past,
Knowing who it was and in the fast
Departing night our hopes and fears depart
Also, one will rise and, from the board, start
To erase the names that confirm...
"One of our aircraft failed to return".

Traditionally we raise our glasses,
Drink a silent toast. A vision passes
Before our eyes, we see the aircraft crash
And scar the pleasant earth. Madly we dash
To the scene, too late, all is charred and black....
"One of our aircraft did not come back".

We see new faces come and go, perchance
We do not realise their significance;
That one day we may also be replaced
And forgotten, as we forgot in haste.
The familiar scene waiting only for
The words ... "We shall see them no more".

**Jim Brookbank**

## REMINISCENCES OF A FISKERTON RUNWAY

In afternoon sunshine, we were walking
Across Lincolnshire meadows one Sunday,
Enjoying the fragrant air and talking,
When, stretched before us, we saw the Runway.

A strip of blue-grey tarmac, flat and wide,
Whose long straight lines narrowed in perspective;
Laid like a mat upon the countryside,
It's two thousand yards subtly deceptive.

Gone are golden acres of ripened wheat
Whose ears languidly waved in each warm breeze.
Instead, a man-made ribbon of concrete
Converges towards the remotest trees.

Past furrowed fields where once a farmer sowed
And harvested his barley, beet and rye;
Through clover pasture goes this wondrous road
That leads to nowhere but the boundless sky.

Now empty huts and hangers stand around
The edge of what was once the aerodrome;
Deserted haunts of those who knew this ground,
Between their exploits, as a home from home.

Mute stone! - what might be your epic story
Of comings and goings, aircraft and crews,
Take-offs and landings; of unknown glory,
Flame-flecked dawns, or anxious hours without news?

What tales could you tell of the few, detailed
For noonday strafe or nocturnal attack
Up in Hell's blue heights, cloudless and contrailed,
Duelling with fighters and diving from flak?

At the start, green lamps flashing 'go', and bands
Of spectators gathered to bid God-speed
To their squadron comrades, with upraised hands,
Forced smiles, and silent prayers which some would need.

Black bombers burdened with missiles and men;
Where are they now? - those whom you safely bore
Into the sunset, climbed Eastwards, and then
Steered for danger and were heard of no more.

Taunting the dark, unfriendly and trackless,
You girdled yourself with pinpoints of light,
Blazing a flarepath into the blackness
To guide tired searching eyes out of the night.

When fliers limped home from the tyrant's lair,
No threshold was ever crossed with more zest
Than this path, between the land and the air,
On to which they and their aircraft came to rest.

Those who flew for the last time, scarce hearing
Death's distant summons, paused they to ponder
That the Runway they rose from, unfearing,
Was a bridge between this world and yonder?.

Alone the wind whispers its secrets, and flowers
Alongside bow sadder heads to the sun;
On the horizon, a cumulus towers
Towards the skies where their triumphs were won.

Soon will come twilight, peaceful and planeless;
Silenced forever the war-drums of Mars.
Remains the Runway - down which passed, nameless
And proud, our sons on their way to the stars.

**Sqdn/Ldr. L. R. Hastings (1946)**

## REQUIEM FOR A REAR GUNNER

And should you weep for him, if so inclined,
Then mingle knowledge with your gift of tears,
Bare not your heart alone - unveil your mind
Upon the history of his nineteen years.

He kicked a ball in narrow London streets
Then pedalled groceries round Walthamstow;
He learnt of love in cheaper Gaumont seats,
Set it to jazz-time on his radio.

He had a wife for seven magic nights,
His eyes grew softer in a small hotel;
They shared a dream of London, rich with lights
And all the things that Woolworths has to sell.

He sat, the sergeant-child, among his crew,
And heard with awe the gross Great Man expound
The cult of polish - extol the sacred few
Who'd glistened long and loyally - on the ground.

Against his shaggy head he brushed a sleeve,
Within the barber's shop considered 'pride',
Bought contraceptives in the hope of leave,
Then flew to Nuremburg that night, and died.

**Walter Clapham**

## THE RECRUITING SONG OF THE R.F.C.

I was standing at the corner
When I heard somebody say,
"Come and join the Flying Corps
Come, step along this way.
"I threw my thirty-chest out,
And put my cap on straight,
And walked into the office
Along with Jack, my mate.

They offered me two bob a day,
I said, "I didn't think,"
But when they murmured "Four bob,"
I said, "Come, have a drink.
"And now I spend my Sundays
With Lizzie in the Lane.
I wonder when I'll get my first
Or see an aeroplane.

I never was so well off
In all my naturel:
You should see me in St. James's,
I am an awful swell.
And now I've been to Larkhill
My education is complete.
"Form fours," "Bout turn," "Two deep,"
Oh! don't I do it neat!

You should see us hold our heads up
When the others pass us by.
The girls they all run after us
And, breathless, say, "Oh, my!
Dear Tommy brave, I'll be your slave,
If you will take me up".
But hastily I answer,
I've an invitation out to sup.

**R.F.C. (Larkhill 1915)**

## REMEMBERING SUMMER 1944

Early mist and song of lark,
Drowned by Koffman Starters bark,
Intakes flaming as props turn,
"Switches off Quick" - douse the burn;
Tiffies clearing brutish throats
Next to rippling field of oats.

Quiet the drome when kites away,
Count them back - all O.K.
Around the cookhouse, bikes a-littering;
Inside, serving, Waaf cooks tittering.

Out on bikes in evenings clear
Seeking for the pubs with beer,
Snooty Waafs driving cars,
Canucks with O. Henry bars.

Runways shimmering in the heat,
Fordson tractor's scorching seat,
Waiting erks of every trade,
Lying cool in the mainplane's shade.
Voices strong, opinions airing;
Friendly disputes, laughter sharing.

Sleeping by the phone at night
Early call, brew tea for Flight
Readiness board and squeak of chalk
In the Flight tent, late night talk.

Straw haired Yanks in hurtling jeeps,
Army ordnance piled in heaps,
Lanes concealing trucks and men,
Trained for D Day, wondering when?

On June the sixth, engines thunder;
Aircraft waves are watched with wonder.
News on Naafi set at night,
Some good, some bad, no easy fight,
Often Tiffies coming back
Badly holed by Jerry flack.

Named as 2nd TAF reserve
We strut around with casual verve,
Expecting move, give books away
Tensed up, waiting for the day.

Then plans to send us over Channel
Are changed "It's pukka gen - no flannel
Me to York, a Ferry flight",
Cushy posting, admit delight.

No liberating now for me...
A different path by chance decree,
But down the years, now past two score,
I remember the Summer of '44.

**Ray Gates (Hurn)**

## SCRAMBLE

An ominous click in the Tannoy, commands instant alert,
All freeze in what they're doing, from the C. O. down to an erk.
'Red section scramble to Dover, climb up to Angels Twenty,
Bandits approaching from the East, for each of you there's plenty'.

Three figures spring in unison, grabbing helmets as they dash,
A Very light shoots skywards to burst in a brilliant red flash.
Three Merlins roar together, wheels straining to jump the chocks,
'Chutes are buckled, mikes plugged in, as across the field they rock.

Lined up together into wind, formed into Vic of three,
A Green fired from the tower, they're off to Hell or victory.
Hoods and undercarts well secured, oil pressures and trim alright,
Must stay together in steady climb, keeping formation tight.

'Hello Tower - Red Section airborne - switching over to Channel B',
'Good hunting Red Section Leader, we will expect you home for tea'
Cathedral towers of Canterbury appear down far below,
Ahead the North Sea gleaming as it meets the Channel's flow.

O'er North Foreland veer starboard ten, turning to due South,
Behind them the Essex shore, there Thames with gaping mouth
At last they spot their quarry, twenty Junkers in tight formation,
Three thou' below, no top cover, a wonderful invitation.

Tally-Ho! and down they go, picking off those in the rear, Surprising
the Hun from the sun, causing a widow's tear
Reflector sights switched on, buttons turned from 'Safe' to 'Fire',
Closing for short bursts, to give our guests a funeral pyre.

Cordite fumes fill cockpits with sulphur stench of Hell,
Two burning Junkers, smoke indicating where they fell.
Spits climb again together, firing from positions below,
Allowing for deflection, they have been taught by those who know.

The trio now form up again, triumphantly making back to base,
Glowing with satisfaction of the successful hunter in the chase.
This day was theirs, German families to feel the sorrow,
Who knows if the Victors will be vanquished on the morrow?

**Len Hurle (1941)**

## SKY OVER HOLLAND

When I look at the sky over Holland at night,
The blue dome and the stars are tranquil and bright.
It is peaceful and still; not a sound to be heard
But the rustling of leaves and the cry of a bird.

Not a bomber, no fighters on high any more,
And no criss-crossing searchlights as in days of war.
All is peaceful and still, for the Germans have gone,
For the battle for freedom was finally won.

When we sat in the path of the bombers at night,
We felt anxious but glad for, their every flight
Brought nearer the day when the Germans would flee,
When the war would be over, and we would be free.

We all prayed with great fervour and often cried out
"Oh Lord keep them safe, let them quickly dive out
Of the crossroads of searchlights high up in the sky,
And please - save their lives God - Oh don't let them die".

The young children prayed: "Send us so many planes
That the sparrows can't fly and must walk in the lanes"
And the parents prayed: "Please, let them soon free us all
From the Teutons' mad fury that holds us in thrall".

Though so many were lost in the terrible fight,
While we prayed and watched anxiously many a night,
Their endeavours and courage have not been in vain,
For by them and their comrades, the Germans were slain.

When I looked at the sky over Holland last night,
The blue dome and the stars were all tranquil and bright.
There is peace, no more sirens, I hear a bird call;
Oh we thank you dear airmen - may God bless you all.

**Maria Ten-Horn (Holland)**

## A FLIGHT ENGINEER

Six pounds the set I'm asking, said the salesroom auctioneer
For the medals of an airman, a Flight Engineer
No one very special, that I do concede
His name is one of many inscribed at Runnymede
Six pounds for the set you say, I think thats rather dear
For the medals of an airman, a Flight Engineer.

**Ken Forester (90 Sqdn)**

## GREMLINS

This is the tale of the Gremlins
Told by the P.R.U.
At Benson and Wick and St. Eval
And believe me, you slobs, it's true.

When you're seven miles up in the heavens
And that's a hell of a lonely spot,
And it's fifty degrees below zero,
Which isn't exactly hot.

When you're frozen blue like your Spitfire,
And you're scared a Mosquito pink,
When you're thousands of miles from nowhere,
And there's nothing below but the drink.

It's then you will see the gremlins,
Green and gamboge and gold,
Male and female and neuter,
Gremlins both young and old.

It's no good trying to dodge them,
The lesson you learned on the link
Won't help you evade a Gremlin
Though you boost and you dive and you jink.

White ones will wiggle your wing-tips,
Male ones will muddle your maps,
Green ones will guzzle your Glycol,
Females will flutter your flaps.

Pink ones will perch on your perspex,
And dance pirouettes on your prop.
There's one spherical middle-aged gremlin
Who spins on your stick like a top.

They'll freeze up your camera shutters,
They'll bite through your aileron wires,
They'll cause your whole tail to flutter,
They'll insert toasting forks in your tyres.

This is the song of the gremlins
As sung by the P.R.U.
Pretty ruddy unlikely to many,
But fact, none the less, to the "Few".

**A P.R.U. Pilot (1942)**

## THE SQUADRON REUNION

Today we are gathered together
In friendship and memories tied,
Remembering when we were just youngsters,
Our characters raw and untried.

We were young and naive and bewildered,
But we learnt very fast to be men,
And for us all the years of our lifetime
Would never be like it again.

Our friendships were forged on the anvil
Of terror, of fire and of flame,
We did what we must without question
Of who was, or was not, to blame.

As did thousands of others just like us
Who battled and suffered and died,
We were not all the same race or nation
Or fighting upon the same side.

And now we remember with gladness
The faces and friends that we knew,
It is pleasant, heart-warming and lovely,
But that is not all we must do.

Thc past was a timc for bcginning
To build up this bonus we've earned,
Yet we cannot, we must not, live in it,
But use all the truths we have learned.

To hold out our hands in true friendship
To those who are lonely and old,
To men of all nations among us,
To a world that is weary and cold.

Maybe it would help in a small way
To make hate and violence cease,
And ensure that we leave to our children
A future of love and of peace.

**Audrey Grealy (1985)**

**SWINDERBY**

Six weeks spent at Swinderby was six weeks of pure Hell,
Physical and mental torture - all the Sergeants did was yell.
Shoes we'd studiously bulled for hours were thrown across the room,
And we'd all quake in our boots when we heard that loud voice boom.

Half an hour it use to take to make that bed pack square,
But unless it was just perfect it went right in the air.
Toilets and showers we scrubbed, rooms we polished top to toe,
But was it ever good enough? The simple answer "No".

The Drill was pretty hard if you've no co-ordination,
"Swing those arms, dig those heels" right around the Station.
Physical Training was another thing, I'm glad I got fit before,
Because if you don't pass your BFT, they'll shout even more.

Ground Defence Training was not too bad & Weapons was good fun,
But the CS Gas in that chamber just made our eyes and noses run.
First Aid Training I didn't like; a Nurse for sure I'll never be,
Blood, guts and broken bones are not for squeamish me!.

Classroom studies were tiresome, they made our eyes slowly close,
But consequences weren't too good if the instructors saw us doze!.
There's just one thing they fail to mention down at the CIO,
That for eighteen hours a day you're constantly on the go.

A lot of people got homesick and a lot of people cried,
Because there were no "Congratulations", however hard we tried.
They did their best to grind us down, to see how much we'd take,
I didn't let them get to me, this was my career at stake.

But eventually the time did pass and my training was complete;
They'd changed my life completely, I'd said good-bye to Civvy Street.
The day I passed out was brilliant, tears came trickling from my eyes,
That wonderful feeling of proudness, made the whole 6 weeks worthwhile.

**SACW Laura Jeffreys (Falklands)**

**THE SQUADRON SAR'MAJOR**

Under the spreading hangar roof
The Sergeant-major stands-
A fierce, imposing monster he,
All quake at his commands-
And the thunder of his booming voice
Is worse than German bands.

His hair is cropped beyond recall
His face is like a boot,
His brow is wet with thoughts of debt
Incurred when a recruit.
He looks nobody in the face,
If so, they have to scoot!

He goes at mid-day to the Mess,
And sits among the swells,
Then drags defaulters by the neck,
And dumps them in the cells,
Whilst his massive fists are tightly clenched
Like those of Billy Wells!

Week in, week out, from morn till night
You can hear him curse the day
When he took-off on his maiden flight
And a beastly strut gave way,
When (according to his own account )
He was foremost in the fray!

Straffing, abusing, bellowing,
Onward through life he goes
Each morning he contrives to add
To many an A.M's woes.
Something attempted, someone "run"
Will earn him a damaged nose!

**Royal Flying Corps (1916)**

## THE OLD BASE

Watchtower in a field of corn
Crumbling Nissens - so forlorn
Hangars used for storing wood
Barley where the Mess once stood
What memories still linger here!
Comradeship and Waafs and beer
Engines roaring with such might
Friends who vanished in the night
Bravery and gripping fear
What memories still linger here!

**Ken Forester (90 Sqdn)**

## STAND THOSE THREE TOWERS

Stand those three towers still a-pointing
In the dawn light, stark and clear?
Does the ghostly roar of the 'Lanc' still soar
O'er the fields of Lincolnshire?

Do the shades of Ancient Briton;
Of Roman, Saxon, Dane;
Still stand and gaze in mute amaze
On the ghosts who throng the plain?

Ghosts of the flower of England;
Of Empire and Allied Kin;
Are they still in sight in the darkening light
Each dusk as the night rolls in?

Ghosts of Geordie, Scouse and Cockney,
Of Yellowbelly and Tyke;
Do they fly again over Martin Fen;
O'er Grimsby and Boston Dyke?

And of Paddy, Jock and Taffy;
Of Aussie, Canuck and Yank.
Are they flying still over Lindum Hill,
O'er the Wash and the Humber Bank?

And the Freedom Men of Europe;
New Zealand and Afric' dark;
Do they still fly strong to the Merlin's song
And the sound of the Browning's bark?

Do those hosts of glad young warriors
Still soar and fly and toil
And fight and die in an alien sky;
Still rest in an alien soil?

Ah! many the distant lonely cross
And many the shattered 'plane
Whose last home sight on a bombers' night
Was a view of a Lincoln Lane.

Does that lumbering bus still rumble
Those lanes from - Thorpe to - by?
Does it still stop hard by the old churchyard
Where more of our brothers lie?

Sons of all the warring nations;
The plain men and the brave.
All troubles past; they've found their last
Safe home in an English grave.

While we, whom they've left behind them;
We few, as our years grow old
Still fight and fly in their battle sky
In dreams when the night is cold.

Ah! Lincoln! Our shire of memories
From the dawn to the setting sun;
Your heath and fen will live again
With us till our journey's run.

**Victor Cavendish**

## STIRLINGS HOMEWARD BOUND

The cold and empty vaults of space
And scudding clouds, alone bear trace,
Or witness now the stirring sound
Of monster aircraft, homeward bound,
Huge, darkened shapes, that grace the gloom,
Beneath the slowly waning moon
Cast, far upon the sea below
Their shadows, in an eerie glow.

For Heaven hath seen no peace this night,
But blazing earth and blinding light
Have spread abroad, where bad men dwell,
And cast thelr spirits into Hell,
To terminate their rule of sin,
And smash defended strongholds in,
To seek their every wicked lair,
Then pulverize it, from the air.

O'er seaborne mist, now droning home,
The Stirlings in their lofty throne
Speed, lightly laden through the dawn,
As night is past, and day is born;
Now some, with gaping wounds are rent,
From stem to stern all holed and bent,
And some with shattered wings, stlll fly
Trlumphant down the moonlit sky.

**George Henfrey (1940)**

## TAIL END CHARLIE DOES HIS BIT

The bomber slowly turned on course
and flew towards the east.
The moon shone on that throbbing force
and beautified the beast.

The bombs hung heavy in their wombs
the bomb sight working well;
Soon to give birth to rubble tombs
in a city's living hell.

Tail end Charlie, testing guns
fired bullets to the sea.
In jubilance raised his thumbs
then gave the Victory 'V'.

Up came the searchlights piercing glare
holding the rolling plane.
Tail end Charlie screamed a prayer
as Death called out his name.

The plane shook off - the blinding ray;
the target flares were red.
"Steady-steady - bombs away!,
Hey skipper' - Charlie's dead"!

Landed - waiting with their kit,
the crew re-lived their fray.
"Have to tell his Cambridge 'bit'-
she's in the family way".

Some hurried off towards the mess
to try to break the strain -
To sing a ribald song,
to stress that they could fly again.

"Anyone seen Charlie - in the Sergeants Mess?
his girl friends mother rung to say,
and he will no doubt guess
the baby is on the way".

**Frank Clear (1944 - 62 Ops)**

## MORNING VIGIL

Empty dispersals at misty dawn
Hoar frost glistening
Groundcrew huddled faces drawn
Listening! Listening!
Waiting for Harry, Stan and Jack
Mid upper Taffy and rear gunner Mac
And young Tommy the engineer
Who could never hold his beer
They were never coming back
Fallen to Texel Flak
Their grave the icy cold North Sea
Vanished for all eternity.

**Ken Forester (90 Sqdn)**

## AN AIRFIELD REMEMBERS

I lie here still beside the hill
Abandoned long to nature's will
My buildings down, my people gone
My only sound the wild birds song.

But my mighty birds will rise no more
No more I hear the Merlins roar
And never now my bosom feels
The pounding of their giant wheels.

From the ageless hill their voices cast
Thunderous echoes of the past
And still in lonely reverie
Their great dark wings sweep down to me.

Laughter, sorrow, hope and pain
I shall never know these things again
Emotions that I came to know
Of strange young men so long ago.

Who knows, as evening shadows meet
Are they with me still, a phantom fleet?
And do my ghosts still stride unseen
Across my face so wide and green.

And in the future, should buildings tall
Bury me beyond recall
I shall remember them
My metal birds, and long dead men.

**Via 49 Sqdn Association**

## TEN LITTLE FIGHTER BOYS

Ten little Fighter boys taking off in line
One was in coarse pitch, and then there were nine
Nine little fighter boys climbing "through the gate"
One's petrol wasn't on, then there were eight
Eight little fighter boys scrambling up to Heaven
One weaver didn't and then there were seven
Seven little fighter boys up to all the tricks
One had a hangover then there were six
Six little flghter boys milling over Hythe
One's pressure wasn't up and then there were five
Five little fighter boys over France's shore
One flew reciprocal and then there were four
Four little fighter boys joining in the spree
One's sight wasn't on and then there were three
Three little fighter boys high up in the blue
One's rubber pipe was loose then there were two
Two little fighter boys homing out of sun
Flew straight and level and then there was one
One little fighter boy happy to be home
Beat up dispersal and then there was none
Ten litte Spitfires nothing have achieved
A.O.C. at Group is very very peeved
Fifty thousand Smackers thrown down the drains
'Cause ten silly baskets didn't use their brains.

**W. Hooper (1942)**

## TO MY WELLINGTON BOMBER

When first we met I felt afraid,
You looked so cumbersome and staid;
Standing quietly near some trees,
Shuddering gently in the breeze
It seemed incredible to me,
That you and I would ever see
Vast tracts of German territory.

Do you remember our first flight?
Climbing steadily through the night.
We went to Bremen, I believe -
Or was it Kiel or Ludenschieve?
But anyhow I could surmise
That in spite of your great size,
You loved your element, the skies.

Then other raids that we went through,
Each one an epic, each one new;
Each one filled with thrills and fears,
Sweating - sick - and near to tears.
Emden shot us up to hell,
Hamburg, Gladbach, Koln as well,
Still, we came home our tales to tell.

But, as before, on frenzied nights,
You steeply dived - while curving lights
Of tracer shells ripped through your frame,
Though cheating death brought us no fame.
And if one night we don't return,
There'll be another star to burn
Brighter than the rest descending
Reflecting on the clouds and lending
Glorious colours to our ending.

**G.E. Radford**

## IN THE LOCAL

You see them in the "Local" anywhere
In town or country near a fighter station
In flying boots and scarves - their ruffled hair
Like schoolboys out for a jolly celebration:
Eight in a car for four had raced along
And miracles were wrought to bring them here.
To pass an hour with banter, darts and song
And drink a pint or two of English beer,
And talk of "binds" and "dims" with lots of natter
Of "ropey jobs" and "wizard types" and "gen"
Amid much laughter glasses chink and clatter.
Deep underneath was hid the real men,
Who saw their comrades fall out of the skies,
And knew too well the look in dead men's eyes.

**W.A.G. Kemp**

**THEY ALSO ..........**

The Lancasters were home to roost,
All shot about and short on boost.
Lucky crews who'd made their stations;
Jangled nerves, recriminations.

"The doofer flange is on the blink.
Nearly dumped us in the drink!
Get it fixed - and double quick !"
Angry words from P.O. Stick.

A.C. Plonk at once obeyed
Though over-worked and under-paid.
He grafted on against the odds
With barely time for char and wads.

Frozen fingers, driving rain;
Cuts and bruises, oaths and pain.
Change the pump and sign the chit
Work with spanners that don't fit.

"No, no", barked Stick, "it's still not right.
The sprangle sprocket's far too tight.
And more than that, the drimble drum
Is all from here to Kingdom Come ".

"I'll fix it, sir," said A.C. Plonk.
"There's end play on the gimblegonk.
We'll have to take the drakshaft out
And shim the nifter. there's no doubt".

Sure, P.O. Stick got terse and bitter,
Balling - out his engine fitter;
Called him idle, called him dim
But in the air thanked God for him.

**Christopher Deardon**

**TEARS ALL THE WAY**

I remember Dortmund, Osterfield, Cologne,
The probing fire of 88s,
The searing searchlight cone,
I remember Gelsenkirchen, Dusseldorf, Berlin,
The pyrotechnic tracer
And the fighters closing in.

Dessau, Scholven, Bremen, I recollect them well:
We bombed them from the Heavens,
From the ground they gave us hell.
I remember watching
As the sullen bonfires grew,
And with them flowered the bitterness
Of those we never knew;

But now though man has long rebuilt
These devastated places,
I fancy they are haunted still
By pale forgotten faces;
The shades of those who felt the fear
And lunacy of war;
Who understood its agony
But not what it was for.

**Philip Nicholson**

## POEM FOR V E DAY

I remember the threat of invasion, when Britain stood alone
Ready to fight to the bitter end, for each Hamlet, field and home.

I remember the Pilots of Britain fighting their last ditch stand
Gaining the vital Air Victory that kept hope within our hand.

I remember the long six year battle fought by Bomber Command
That broke the strength of the enemy and cracked their evil plan.

I remember the Army and Navy and their battles with the foe
The Blitzes, the Civilian spirit, all through the war it flowed.

I remember the hundreds of thousands who died against the foe
Content to even give their lives that in Freedom our kids could grow.

I remember when war came to its end in 1945
How people laughed and sang in relief and how so many cried.

I remember that War for Freedom and our gallant Bulldog Breed
They gave back freedom to Europe and nations of all creeds.

I remember the sacrifice for Victory, so let us honour that day
Let us raise our glasses to Victory and Freedom - but also let us Pray!.

**Jim Davis (VE Day - 1945)**

## OPEN LETTER TO A BLACK MARKETEER

DEAR SIR: I have the pleasure to observe
That one inspired court has found it fit
To pass a three-years' sentence on yourself;
My friends hope you'll enjoy it quite a bit!
These friends, I may remark, are simple folk
Whose conversation runs from "kites" to "flak."
For twelve-and-six a day they do a trip
From which a fair percentage don't come back!
It seems to me a very curious thing
That these young people's chance of growing old
Is made to guarantee the privilege
Of helping such as you amass your gold!
Well, let that rest.... But would some witchcraft grant
To you, what time you're pacing in your cell,
Imagination of a poet's sort,
And as things are, we'd have you then, in hell!

**Anthony Richardson**

## THREE CHEERS FOR THE MAN ON THE GROUND

Wherever you walk, you will hear people talk,
Of the men who go up in the air.
Of the dare-devil way, they go into the fray;
Facing death without turning a hair.

They'll raise a big cheer and buy lots of beer,
For a pilot who's home on leave;
But they don't give a jigger,
For a flight mech, or rigger
With nothing but 'props' on his sleeve.

They just say 'Nice day' and then turn away,
With never a mention of praise.
And the poor bloody erk who does all the work;
Just orders his own beer, and pays!

They've never been told of the hours in the cold
That he spends sealing Germany's fate.
How he works on a kite, till all hours of the night,
And then turns up next morning at eight.

He gets no rake-off for working 'till take-off;
Or helping the aircrew prepare;
But whenever there's trouble, it's 'Quick at the double',
The man on the ground must be there.

Each flying crew could tell it to you;
They know what this man's really worth.
They know he's a part of the RAF's heart,
Even though he stays close to the earth.

He doesn't want glory, but please tell his story:
Spread a little of his fame around.
He's one of a few, so give him his due;
Three cheers for the man on the ground.

**E. Sykes (1942)**

## TOUR EXPIRED

Into the village of Sutton I drove,
To my old favourite pub, called "The Brook"
And I sat reminiscing of hours spent with friends,
Who had logged their last op' in their book.
They would say their goodbyes in the morning,
Perhaps never to meet again,
But the bond that had bound them together,
Through this life would always remain.
The custom of feet on the ceiling
Performed with much gusto and pride,
As the pilot would pen his name to the marks,
As emotion the crew tried to hide.
For this was their last night together,
Come the dawn they would all go their ways,
With only their memories to cherish
Of "The Crew" and "The Old Flying Days".
The door of The Brook I threw open;
The landlord was one and the same,
I looked at the ceiling and said; "Its been done"
And he jokingly called me a name.
"You're one of the lads who flew from the drome!"
I nodded my head with a smile.
"Welcome back" he said with some feeling,
"I haven't seen you for a while"
The barman poured me a lager
And said: "I was up there like you"
So I gave him an old battle-order
To show when exiles came through.

**Ken Moore (75 Sqdn)**

## TAIL END ALBERT

Ah'll tell thee a tale of young Albert,
What'e did up aloft all alone,
In t'tail of a Halifax bomber,
What went on a raid to Cologne.
T'ground crew 'ad spent all the mornin'
In stuffing up aircraft wi' bombs;
T'crew put on all their warm clothing
(Young Albert 'ad two pair of combs).
A comical figure was Albert
By time preparations were done;
E'd 'is stick with its 'orses 'ead 'andle
To poke out through t'ole in 'is gun.

E'ad 'elmet and goggles and gauntlets,
Flyin' boots, fur lined suit and Mae West;
'is pockets 'ed stuffed full of 'umbugs,
'E'd a large parachute on his chest.
When 'e tried to get into 'is turret,
'E were too wide t' go through the 'ole;
T'Engineer Officer had to be summoned
To lever 'im in with a pole.
T'Bomber took off rather sudden,
Young Albert were sortin' 'is gear,
When turret floor came up and 'it 'im
An 'ell of a clout on 'is ear.

When t'bomber were over the target,
Young Albert came to with a start,
For a sample from Krupp's works at Essen
'Ad 'it 'im in tenderest part.
This were not altogether surprisin'
For as soon as the bombing begun
The 'ole of the Germans defences,
Was chucking up muck by the ton.
At that moment up came a night-fighter,
Albert's mouth became suddenly dry,
So 'e popped in a ruddy great 'umbug,
Shut 'is eyes, took 'is aim and let fly.

Pilot shouted, "Whats 'e doin at back end?"
When 'e 'eard gun go off like a blizzard,
In reply Albert did nowt but gurgle,
'Umbug 'ad stuck in 'is gizzard.
'E kept firin' 'is gun at the fighter,
While 'e coughed and endeavoured to talk,
When all of a sudden the 'umbug
Shot out of 'is mouth like a cork.

Jerry pilot were all unsuspectin'
Of missile approaching its goal,
T'umbug then struck 'im on t'side of 'is noddle
And 'is aircraft fell out of control.
"Oh good show" said 'is Pilot to Albert,
"There ain't no other gunner like thee,
And when we get back to the airfield,
Ah'll give thee an egg for thi' tea".

But when they got back they discovered,
That there weren't no hegg to be 'ad,
So they went to consult the Group Captain
As to 'ow to reward the brave lad.
D.F.M. it were not thought sufficient,
They were all in a bit of a jam,
Till at last they decided to give 'im
A lovely great plateful of Spam.

**Harry Holmes (218 Sqdn)**

## THAT THING - THE BARRACUDA

Why should the unoffending sky,
Be tainted and corrupted by
This product of a twisted brain,
That's aeronautically insane,
This vile and hideous abortion,
Devoid of beauty and proportion,
That people call a Barracuda,
Whose form is infinitely cruder
Than any other scheme or plan
As yet conceived by mind of man.
To see it stagger into space
Would bring a blush upon the face,
Of the most hardened Pharisee
Within the aircraft industry.
But I suggest we don't decry
This winged horror of the sky;
But keep it 'til the War is won,
And then we'll all join in the fun.
Festoon the wings with fairy lights
And wheel it out on gala nights,
Thus so we'll help dispel the rumour
That Britons have no sense of humour.

**F.A.A. Officer**

## WAITING TO START ENGINES

Five more minutes of silence -
five more minutes to the green flare
and the roar of Hercules.
Five minutes sitting quietly
secure in straps and in the neat familiarity
of a hundred dials,
each in its known place
and all of them still:
none yet calling for action or anxiety.
Time to put the chocolate
in its usual place,
stow the coffee flask,
settle the map,
arrange the flying suit
comfortably in the creases of the crutch
confirm the tanks are full:
take turn among other voices
calling from perspex cells
to check the tower.
"Sunray from Plumbird Seven -
How do you read?"

Two minutes more.
Threatened with engines
the silence tightens.
Beyond the armoured glass
the grass is green,
the sky is less than one tenth cirro-cu:
tenders, tractors, people, other planes
stand very still
waiting their moment in the summer field:
the quick transparent wave of asphalt heat
is all that moves ...

And then it strikes -
this breakout from the skull
this bayonet thought
pierces the bowels
and the body floods
with knowledge
of this cockpit broken,
the sight, the sound, the smell
of death and broken dials.
of torn flesh
and self no longer self
crumpled in metal.

A minute yet to the flare.
A minute to run with the wind
and flow with the mothering tide
past fitters and riggers,
red eyed among chocks,
to bend with the bending hawthorns
at the airfield's edge.

**Phil Brett (1944)**

## AN ODE TO THE U-BOATS

O, slinky, slimy, slithering snake,
You make poor trawlers quiver and quake,
But following your elusive feather
In every kind of dirty weather,
In rain or hail, snow or fine
Come those who'll catch you - 269.

You hide beneath the waters green,
But we will find you, submarine.
Although you in our channels lurk
To try to do your dirty work,
That death-portending screaming whine
Means you've been seen by 269.

Your conning tower, that glorious sight
Comes into view just on the right.
The bombs are live, the eye is keen
Crash-dive you cowardly submarine,
This bomb will break your slinky spine -
A job well done by - 269.

Now, submarine, take this to heart,
When your next raid is due to start,
Your chance is NIL; the odds too great;
So shoot yourself; it's not too late.
If you're not blown up by a mine
You sure will be by 269.

**B Flight (269 Sqdn)**

## A WAAF AT BRIDGENORTH

Wooden huts in rows so tidy
Homesick thoughts beneath the hills
Narrow iron beds we hide in
Bright the lino polished floors.

Stifled yawns at morning lecture
Rubber stench at gas-mask drill
Whispered jokes and pangs of hunger
Long the queue for dining hall.

Eager march to stores for fitting
Uniforms we proudly don
Underwear for active service?
Vanity and frills begone.

Shoes and buttons, badges shining
Floor and metal polish smell
Tannoy's interrupting whining
"Attention all WAAF personnel".

All too soon the time for leaving
Hills and huts and shining floor
Kit inspected; Pay Paraded
Final march to guardroom door.

Filled with bright anticipation
All aglow with shining brass
Pray salute us, proudly passing
Aircraft Women, second class!.

**Kathleen Chamont (1942)**

## TRUE LOVE

I remember when in early teens, I had my first affair
I fell so helplessly in love and many nights we shared
I remember how often she brought me home, when I was worse for wear
And how often her strength would comfort me when I was in despair.

She was sturdy with delightful curves, a really lovely sight
Although dressed drab, she often shone, especially at night
Her name became so popular, men adored her from afar
They came in thousands to take her out beneath the glittering stars.

I was content to share my love with all these other men
I knew how they were under her spell, I felt the very same
She was the loveliest lady we'd ever met, and the day we had to part
It created an absence never filled and broke a thousand hearts.

She was told "Your no longer needed" so she gracefully retired
She no longer took out eager young men and made them all perspire
She made so many boys into men she took all in her stride
When she was gone I'm sure many of her admirers cried.

I have not seen her for many years and now I'm getting on
But still I can see her splendid shape and hear her throbbing song
Men of all nations loved her, regardless of creed or rank
Remember the nights you spent with your love, your dear old Lanc!.

**Jim Davis (1950)**

## WHERE ARE THEY NOW?

Where are they now who once wore Air Force blue,
Who flew into that awful living hell
To sacrifice their precious, golden lives,
Then tightly hold us in their timeless spell.

The records may tell us they live no more -
Not so, not so! We would swiftly reply.
'Missing' and 'Dead' are just meaningless words,
For in our hearts they simply cannot die.

If you can remember the smiling babe
However can you doubt he still lives on?
If you can yet recall the laughing child
However can you think of him as gone?

If you still share thoughts with husband or son,
Or sweetheart, or cousin, or a friend,
If you feel they are never far away,
Deep in your heart they'll live on without end.

Time has done nothing to take them away,
They are as loved as they have ever been.
Now Fiskerton has recorded them with pride
And keeps our precious memories evergreen.

Where are they now? We do not need to ask.
While our hearts beat and memorials remain
They live on and stay close to every one of us -
Though we shall not see their like again.

**K. J. Lucas (Fiskerton 1987)**

## WAITING

Sun, sand and smells
and no mail from home
Back to the compound
to have a good moan.
Conflict is over the battle is won
Now we wait to get started
on our way home.
No khaki drill skirts,
ankle socks or black sandals
Back to hot baths
and loos with flush handles.
To arms held to greet us
and tears to be shed
for those of our loved ones
who are maimed or known dead.
Who can claim victory
for losing a son
Pray God, give us peace
for all time to come.

**LACW Molly Watts (Cairo)**

## AT A PARTY

FOREMOST, the ribbon on your breast they saw,
And then the added braid upon your arm,
Praising a fate protecting you from harm,
(What caused old Death to fumble at your door?)
Nor any looks of yours resemblance bore
To one who'd gazed past life! Your studied calm
Was but the varnish to that pictured charm-
The usual decoration that you wore!
How should they guess that, yet, you had to kill
Those groping, grey cold thoughts and come to grips
With what would paralyse your stubborn will
Before you ventured forth on further trips?
Was I alone to know a cup can fill,
And watch the anguish of your laughing lips?

**Anthony Richardson**

## WHAT THINK YOU, AIRMAN?

What think you, airman, when you fly
So proudly there in heaven's sky?
Do you exalt in your great might,
As you go onward through the night?
I think of death beneath my wings,
And the dire load my bomber brings;
My spirit flinches from the thought
That of this carnage may come naught.
I pray that soon the day will come
When man will offer man his hand,
And peace prevail throughout the land.
I face up to my moment's task
And three things alone of God I ask,
Please help my flesh to stand the strain
Protect us, Lord, this once again;
And if this cannot be your plan,
Give me the strength to be a man.

**Dennis Hornsey**

## "BOMBER" HARRIS'S STONE

The "Bombers" stone is splattered red
They come to vilify our dead,
Yet in our time of deepest trouble
The nation cheered them from the rubble.

Flak and fighter, shell torn skin
Telegrams to Next of Kin,
Not one thousand but fifty five
And many of whom were burned alive.

Its right to forget
its right to forgive,
But remember they died
That you might live.

May the attack on the "Bomber" cease
May the Bomber Boys rest in peace,
Many had no grave they had no plot
The "Bombers" stone was all they got.

**Bill Driscoll (1993)**

**THE YANKEE INVASION**

Dear Old England is not the same.
We dreaded invasion, and yet it came.
But though it's not the beastly Hun
The gosh darn Yankee army's come.

You see them in the tram and bus.
There isn't any room for us.
We walk to let them have our seats
And get run over by their jeeps.

They moan about our lukewarm beer-
Say beer's like water over here
But after having two or more
You'll find them lying on the floor.

You should see them try to dance.
They grab a partner and start to prance.
When you're half dead, they stop and smile,
Say "How's about it, honey chile."

You see them try to jitterbug.
They twist and turn and pull and hug.
It's enough to make an old Indian jealous,
Yet Yanks are civilized, or so they tell us.

Yankee officers cause us to smile,
With coloured pants seen for miles.
We wonder if they're mice or men,
But decide they're wolves, so avoid the den.

With admiration we do stare
At the ribbons they do wear,
And think of battles brave and daring
That won the ribbons they are wearing.

Alas, they have not fought the Hun.
No furious battles have they won.
That pretty ribbon just denotes
They have crossed the sea, brave men in boats.

They laugh at us for drinking tea,
Yet funnier sight you'll never see
Than a gum-chewing Yank with glum-looking face.
He'd raise a laugh in any place.

We speak to them; they just look hazy.
They think we're nuts; we think they're crazy.
But they're our Allies; we must be nice.
We love them, yes, like cats love mice.

**A WAAF (Mendlesham)**

## SEPULCHRE OF HEROES

Each one, man by man, has won imperishable praise. Each has gained a glorious grave, not that sepulchre of earth within they lie, but the living tomb of everlasting remembrance wherein glory is enshrined, remembrance that will live on the lips that will blossom in the deeds of their countrymen the world over.

For the whole world is the sepulchre of heroes, monuments may rise and tablets be set up to them in their own land, but on far-off shores there is an abiding memorial that no pen, or chisel has traced, it is graven not in stone or brass, but on the living hearts of humanity.

Take these men as your example. Like them, remember that posterity can only be for the free, that freedom is the sure possession of those alone who have the courage to defend it.

**Pericles (425 BC - Military Commander)**

## I AM NOT THERE

Do not stand at my grave and weep,
I am not there, I do not sleep.
I am the thousand winds that blow,
I am the diamond glints on snow.
I am the sunlight on ripened grain,
I am the gentle Autumnal rain.
When you wake to the morning thrush,
I am the soft uplifting rush
of quiet birds in circled flight
I am the soft stars that shine at night
Do not stand at my grave and cry
I am not there - I did not die.

**British Soldier (Northern Ireland)**

## WHERE ARE THEY?

Where are the bombers, the Lancs on the runway,
Snub nosed and roaring and blackfaced and dour,
Full up with aircrew and window and ammo,
And dirty great cookies to drop on the Ruhr?

Where are the pilots, the navs and airgunners,
Wops and bomb aimers and flight engineers.
Lads who were bank clerks and milkmen and teachers,
Carpenters, lawyers and grocers and peers?

Geordies and Cockneys and Wiltshire moonrakers,
Little dark men from the valleys of Wales,
Manxmen, Devonians, Midlanders, Scouses,
Jocks from the Highlands and Tykes from the Dales?

Where are the fliers from Canada's prairies,
From cities and forests determined to win,
Thumbing their noses at Goering's Luftwaffe,
And busily dropping their bombs on Berlin.

Where are the Aussies, the sports and the cobbers,
Talking of cricket and sheilas and grog,
Flying their Lancs over Hamburg and Stettin,
And back to the Lincolnshire winter-time bog?

Where are the Poles with their gaiety and sadness.
All with the most unpronounceable names,
Silently, ruthlessly flying in vengeance,
Remembering their homes and their country in flames?

Where are the Kiwis who left all the sunshine
For bleak windy airfields and fenland and dyke,
Playing wild mess games like high cockalorum,
And knocking the hell out of Hitler's Third Reich?

The Lancs are no more, they are part of the legend,
But memory stays bright in the hearts of the men
Who loved them and flew them through flak and hellfire
And managed to land them in England again.

The men who were lucky to live to see victory,
The men who went home to their jobs and their wives,
The men who can tell their grandchildren with pride
Of the bomber which helped to save millions of lives.

**Audrey Grealy (1982)**

## IT'S BERLIN TONIGHT

It's Berlin tonight - the ''Big City'', that's right.
Memories of dusk with light fading fast.
That nerve soothing fag that could be your last.
The jokes and forced humour; the latest duff rumour.
Dispersals and Lancs - high octane full tanks.
The groups of tense bods who don't fancy the odds.
Sprog crews with the jitters; - last rush job by fitters.
Flying rations and maps; those last minute flaps.
Battledress and warm boots; Sidcot and 'chutes.
Young pilots and crews, beware the main spar's sore bruise.
That deadly bomb bay loaded earlier that day.
The Erks and the Waafs, the Paddys and Taffs.
It's Berlin tonight - the ''Big City'', that's right.

It's a muck sweat to Berlin; now the coughing of Merlins,
That song heard before with its shattering roar.
Watch the shimmering props; light glints from turret tops.
Perspex and metal; young men in fine fettle.
Not eager to go, but it's Berlin and so:
Mae Wests, chewing gum, oranges for some.
Coffee in flasks and oxygen masks.
Mirth that sounds forced, hot crackling exhausts.
Oil pressures and boost engine noise rouse rooks from roost.
Last moments to borrow - and will I see tomorrow?
For it's Berlin tonight - the ''Big City', that's right.

**John Walsh (1988)**

## A TRIBUTE TO THE MEMORIAL FLIGHT

Lancaster, Spitfire, Hurricane;
Names that fill one with pride,
As they take us back down memory lane
To the war and the turn of the tide.

In peace they fly across the sky
On 'Battle of Britain' Day,
To remind us of the reason why
Pure Genius came our way.

**Frank Newton (35, 84 & 206 Sqdns)**

## THE NIGHT BOMBERS

They're busy to-night - the lads of the sky,
They admit to no fear, no price ls too high,
Their engines roar as they take off at night.
The Youth of the Empire - the Guardians of Right.

A thouscnd are heading out to Cologne.
Again the next night - tired to the bone.
We switch on the wireless and what do we learn?
That "some of our aircraft have failed to return".

In the mess they seem carefree - they force the good cheer,
As they each "shoot a line" over bottles of beer.
But up in the air, there's a job to be done.
And the bloodlest battle has yet to be won.

But they'll do it, these lads in their camouflaged kite.
They'll do it for Country, for King and for Right.
For all that is decent and honest and dear,
They'll do it - these lads who never show fear.

Did they flinch at their task? Did they want to turn back
From the enemy fighters, the searchlights and flack?
No, they pressed on to their target, not heeding the price
And fearlessly made the last sacrifice.

And when the day dawns that Church bells start ringing,
When you see people laugh, and you hear people singing,
Just stop to think of the many who'll yearn,
For a gallant young hero "who failed to return".

**P. Bewsher (RCAF)**

## THE HOUSEWIFE'S DREAM

My saucepans have all been surrendered,
The teapot is gone from the hob,
The colander's leaving the cabbage
For a very much different job.

So now, when I hear on the wireless
Of Hurricanes showing their mettle,
I see, in a vision before me,
A Dornier chased by a kettle.

**Elsie Cawser**

## THE LONG FAREWELL

Tangmere is closing down they say,
They've dined the Squadrons out and soon
The wise face of the hunter's moon
Will see them scattered far away.

The old pens where the fighters lay,
Awaiting the marauding Hun,
Lie empty now, like ancient scars
Weed grown beneath the setting sun.

The Squadrons climb against the sky,
Deep-etched against the dying light,
The wind stirs softly, like a sigh,
For those who fly and those who fight.

This field, as famed as Agincourt,
Or Crecy, with their mailed hosts,
Where those who valued freedom fought,
Sleeps, guarded by its valiant ghosts.

**Hannah M. Hunt.**

## THE MOON SHINES BRIGHT

The moon shines bright
On the Ruhr tonight,
A Lancaster makes its attack.
The gunner peers
And controls his fears
That perhaps he won't get back.

The target burns
And the aircraft turns
To avoid the vicious flak.
The gunner grins
As the fighter spins
"I'll be glad when we get back".

With its tanks on fire
The 'Lanc' climbs higher,
A salvo has broken its back.
The gunner dies in these hostile skies
And he won't be coming back!

**Jim Brookbank**

## LISTEN TO THE WIND

Stranger, pause here a little while,
And listen to the West wind's sigh;
With it's tale of long gone men-
Earth shall not see their like again.

Stand by this stone and lend an ear,
And I'll show you ghosts of yesteryear;
The windsock's creak, the cold wind's moan,
Long-dead men crowd around-we're not alone.

Look on this empty, lonely place,
Do their shadows unseen, still cross my face?
Listen, far off thunder-or a Merlin's roar
Borne on the wind, from time's receding shore?

Abandoned, quiet, here I lie,
Time stands still, though years roll by;
Runways broken, dispersals gone,
The only sound a skylark's song.

Half a hundred years have passed,
Half a century since I saw them last;
Lancasters, black against the sky,
Aircrews, young, so many soon to die.

They came from England and far distant shores,
Volunteers, each one, to defend Liberty's just cause;
These fractured runways know how many went,
Silent witness to Youth's blood, spent.

I was created from the very earth for which they fought,
My rich dark soil with their sacrifice, they bought;
In Lincoln Cathedral, yonder, their names are to be found,
And know this-by their blood, you stand on hallowed ground.

Let the tangled weeds that cover me remain,
Shrouding my memories of hope and pain;
And, as I return slowly to the land,
Let this proud stone in perpetual homage stand.

So, Stranger, continue now upon your way,
But forget not those who-it seems but yesterday-
Gave all their tomorrows that you might live,
For **your** freedom, they gave their all they had to give.

**Cedric Keith St George Roberts. (May 1995)**

## THE LAST MAN IN THE AIR FORCE!

I'm the last man left in the Air Force!
In my office inside MoD
I've a copy of Queen's Regulations
Applicable only to me.
I can post myself off to St Mawgan,
Detach me from there to Kinloss,
Or send me on courses to Cosford
Then cancel the lot - I'm the boss.

I'm the last man left in the Air Force!
I suppose you imagine it's great
To be master of all you survey,
But I tell you, it's difficult, mate.
I inspected three stations last Tuesday
As C-in-C (Acting) of Strike,
Then cleaned out the bogs at Brize Norton
And repaired Saxa Vord's station bike.

I'm the last man left in the Air Force!
My wife says I'm never at home.
When I'm not flying kites I'm at Manston
Laying gallons and gallons of foam.
Or I'm in my marine craft off Plymouth
Shooting flares at the crowds on the Hoe,
Or I'm an Orderly Sergeant at Valley.
It's an interesting life - but all go!

I'm the last man left in the Air Force!
When not ADC to the Queen
I'm the Red Arrows leader at Scampton;
I'm the QCS Silent Drill Team.
Tomorrow I'm painting the guardroom
And air testing several planes.
The day after that I'm in London,
Where I'm Chaplain at St Clement Danes.

I'm the last man left in the Air Force!
But I'm pensioned off before long.
There's been no talk of any replacement
And I can't justify signing on.
I hope to enjoy my retirement,
I've put up a fairly good show.
But I won't cut myself off entirely
There are always reunions, you know.

**Harry C. Heywood (W/O, TCC, Grimsby)**

## A FLEMISH FIELD

A field far away, but brought so near
By loving memories we hold so dear,
They were too young, and fresh from the womb,
To end their youth in this grassy tomb.

They flew twenty two, without any fuss,
They flew and fought for the likes of us,
The celestial hanger called out that night,
We are receiving - seven spirits in flight.

Like a wooden cross, stood a single tree,
Looking down on their destiny,
Giving comfort to one of the crew,
His moments left were just a few.

The soldiers came and circled their craft,
Standing sentinel, silent, fore and aft,
Grim faced lads from a foreign land,
Doing a duty, I'll never understand.

The grass grew greener over the years,
Warmed by our love, watered by our tears,
The scar in the soil has long been healed,
Now its a meadow, and a Flemish Field.

I walked alone through that grass to find,
A mark, a sign, for peace of mind,
I looked through time, a void to fill,
Visions came, but I am searching still.

I know it is written, I know its decreed,
But why destroy this happy breed,
Manhood severed, and their fate was sealed,
To greet their Maker in a Flemish Field.

**Eddy Coward (1987)**

# CONCLUSION

In conclusion, what can I say, --- just that compiling this anthology has given me so much pleasure, and if you are disappointed because your own work or your favourite poem is not included, I hope you will forgive me.

I have made an exhaustive search in an attempt to trace the authors of all the poems. In a few cases I have not been successful but have still included their work as the poems in question were too good to be excluded. I will however be only too pleased to hear from anyone whose work I have included that I was not able to contact.

My anthology has been put together, not for the purpose of self recognition or profit, but to share the joy of all these poems with so many readers. A donation will be made to the 49 Sqdn Association (RAF Bomber Command) for every copy of "The Poems We Wrote" that is sold.

I have refrained from encumbering every page with a thumb nail history or an anecdote for each poem, it would only impair your poetic taste buds and spoil the rhythm of the verses.

Should you have any questions relating to the poems in this book, I will be very pleased to answer your letters. Also, new poems for my collection will always be welcome, and who knows, there may be enough material for another anthology ---- "More Poems We Wrote".

My sincere thanks and gratitude go out to two good friends, Les Hay and Ted Cachart for all their valued assistance, encouragement, advice and expertise. Also, my thanks to Max Bygraves for his kind words and interest in my anthology, he paints a vivid picture of Air Force life. Max spent many happy years in the RAF, together with his wife Blossom who served in the WAAF, and they still look back to those days with nostalgia.

I would like to close my anthology with these immortal words of the great Omah Khyyam (1859)

"The moving finger writes, and having writ,
Moves on. Nor all the piety nor wit
Shall lure it back to cancel half a line,
Nor all the tears wash out a word of it".

**Eddy Coward** **1997** **Rayleigh. Essex**

**INDEX**

## INDEX

**INDEX**

## INDEX